Processing

CAUTION
Do Not Demagnetize

Medical Documents

Second Edition

 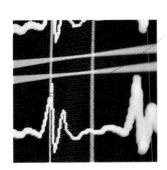  

Robert Poland

Professor Emeritus
Business and Distributive Education
Michigan State University
East Lansing, Michigan

Glencoe
McGraw-Hill

New York, New York   Columbus, Ohio   Woodland Hills, California   Peoria, Illinois

Reviewers

Judy Anderson
Coastal Carolina Community College
Jacksonville, North Carolina

Murlene Asadi
Scott Community College
Davenport, Iowa

Narissa Cadiz-Salvador
Drake Business School
Astoria, New York

Melody Abbott Carlton
Caddo Kiowa Vocational Technical College
Fort Cobb, Oklahoma

Dr. Marty Driggers
South Texas Vo-Tech
Brownsville, Texas

Laura Haberman, R.N.
Christian Star Academy
Mt. Vernon, Ohio

Sara Jane Jones, R.R.A.
Nashville State Technical Institute
Nashville, Tennessee

Loreen W. MacNichol
Andover College
Portland, Maine

Deena Rager
Knox Community Hospital
Mt. Vernon, Ohio

John Kevin Schmelzer
Southeast Business College
Lancaster, Ohio

Wendi Warren
Southwest Technical Center
Altus, Oklahoma

Roberta A. Wyloge
Maric College of Medical Careers
San Diego, California

Library of Congress Cataloging-in-Publication Data
Poland, Robert P.
    Processing medical documents / Robert P. Poland.—2nd ed.
        p.   cm.
    Prev. ed. published with title: Processing medical documents using WordPerfect.
        Includes index.
        ISBN 0-02-804745-1
        1. Medical transcription.   2. WordPerfect (Computer file)
I. Title.
R728.8. P65 1999
651.5'04261'02855369—dc21   98-49590
                                                                    CIP

Glencoe/McGraw-Hill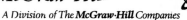
A Division of The McGraw-Hill Companies

Processing Medical Documents, Second Edition

Send all inquiries to:

Glencoe/McGraw-Hill
936 Eastwind Drive
Westerville, Ohio 43081

ISBN 0-02-804745-1

1 2 3 4 5 6 7 8 9   05 04 03 02 01 00 99

Contents

PREFACE V

HAYES MEDICAL CENTER PROCEDURES MANUAL 1

Welcome 1
General Information 2
Supplies 3
Formatting Guidelines 4
Word Division Rules 6
Spacing With Punctuation and Symbols 6
Proofreaders' Marks 8
Formats 9

UNIT 1   ADMISSIONS OFFICE 16

Focus on Medical Careers 16
Objectives 16
Orientation 17
Document Processing: Jobs 1–10 17

UNIT 2   HEAD AND NECK UNIT 28

Focus on Medical Careers 28
Objectives 28
Orientation 29
Document Processing: Jobs 11–22 29

UNIT 3   CARDIOVASCULAR MEDICINE UNIT 40

Focus on Medical Careers 40
Objectives 40
Orientation 41
Document Processing: Jobs 23–34 41

UNIT 4   PLASTIC SURGERY UNIT 56

Focus on Medical Careers 56
Objectives 56
Orientation 57
Document Processing: Jobs 35–45 57

UNIT 5   ALLERGY/IMMUNOLOGY UNIT 66

Focus on Medical Careers 66
Objectives 66
Orientation 67
Document Processing: Jobs 46–57 67

UNIT 6   UROLOGY   78

Focus on Medical Careers 78
Objectives 78
Orientation 79
Document Processing: Jobs 58–65 79

UNIT 7   SURGERY   86

Focus on Medical Careers 86
Objectives 86
Orientation 87
Document Processing: Jobs 66–77 87

UNIT 8   ONCOLOGY   98

Focus on Medical Careers 98
Objectives 98
Orientation 99
Document Processing: Jobs 78–92 99

UNIT 9   DERMATOLOGY   112

Focus on Medical Careers 112
Objectives 112
Orientation 112
Document Processing: Jobs 93–107 112

UNIT 10   INTERNAL MEDICINE   122

Focus on Medical Careers 122
Objectives 122
Orientation 123
Document Processing: Jobs 108–116 123

APPENDIX   134

Skillbuilding 135
Abbreviations 145
Glossary 150
Staff Directory 158
Patient Directory 160
Medicines and Medical Terminology Chart 162
Technical Data Chart 163
Job Profile Charts 165

INDEX   185

Preface

Processing Medical Documents, Second Edition, is an opportunity to create, retrieve, and revise medical documents. You will work in a medical center and rotate through various medical specialty units. You must apply your knowledge of word processing features to complete the various documents accurately and efficiently.

The text contains current medical technology and terminology. The medical data for those units that were part of the first edition of the text were reviewed and updated by the same group of physicians and medical specialists who provided the original data. A number of repetitive jobs were eliminated to incorporate the new data provided by reviewers and to add several new medical specialty units.

The medical data for the new units were gathered from a group of contemporary medical physicians and specialists who diagnosed and prescribed treatment within the past two years for the problems presented in the textbook. Various medical associations, institutions, and instructors also aided in the development of the second edition.

The textbook is organized to progress from a simple to a higher order of planning. Copy is handwritten, typed, rough-draft, and simulated dictation. In the latter part of the course, data must be extracted from verbal and written information to compose documents. Occasionally, reports will be typed on hospital and medical center templates. Throughout the text, responses to human relations and other situations that are characteristic of the medical environment must be resolved and composed.

Language arts and other formatting tips appear in the side margin of the page where appropriate to assist you as you work through the course.

Text Format

A Procedures Manual at the front of the text presents an overview of Hayes Medical Center, its organization, and its staff. In addition, it contains information you should know before you begin working, model documents to help with formatting, word division rules, spacing rules, and a chart of proofreaders' marks.

Each unit opens with a focus on a career in the medical field. Next is a list of unit objectives. The objectives are followed by a list of medical terms associated with the particular office or medical specialty. You may type the terms, spell-check them, and add the appropriate terms to a supplemental dictionary as directed by your instructor.

The second edition of *Processing Medical Documents* includes the following units:

Unit 1	Admissions Office
Unit 2	Head and Neck
Unit 3	Cardiovascular Medicine
Unit 4	Plastic Surgery
Unit 5	Allergy/Immunology
Unit 6	Urology*
Unit 7	Surgery*
Unit 8	Oncology*
Unit 9	Dermatology
Unit 10	Internal Medicine

*New units.

In the back of the text are staff and patient directories, a glossary of medicines and medical terminology, and a list of medical abbreviations.

Following the Index are Medicines and Medical Terminology, Technical Data, and Job Profile Charts for each of the ten units. Use these forms to record information you will use repeatedly throughout the course for reference and to keep track of your work for each unit.

Skillbuilding and Timings

Skillbuilding exercises and timings are provided in the back of the book to aid in building speed and accuracy in typing medical documents. A skillbuilding exercise and timing are correlated to each medical specialty unit.

Data Disk

A Student Data Disk containing templates used in the course is included with this text. Use the templates to create documents and retrieve and revise other documents stored on the disk.

Skills Needed

Processing Medical Documents is an extension of the best-selling *Gregg Keyboarding & Document Processing, 8th Edition,* program (Ober, Hanson, Johnson, Rice, Poland, Rossetti). Anyone who has completed the first two semesters of a keyboarding and document processing course using the *8th Edition* will have learned the prerequisite word processing skills necessary to complete the assignments in *Processing Medical Documents.* A general course in keyboarding plus a word processing course can be substituted for *Gregg College Keyboarding & Document Processing;* however, a knowledge of word processing skills is essential.

Acknowledgments

The author wishes to express his appreciation to the medical specialists, physicians, office assistants, and reviewers who contributed so much to this text.

HAYES MEDICAL CENTER
Procedures Manual

Welcome

Welcome to Hayes Medical Center. We are pleased that you have chosen our health-care facility for your internship. While you work in the Center, you will meet many members of our medical staff as well as our business staff. They will assist in training you and helping you explore careers in health-related occupations.

ORGANIZATION

Hayes Medical Center is one of the top medical centers in the state of Ohio and is affiliated with Memorial Hospital. The Center has many specialty units including allergy and immunology, cardiovascular medicine, dermatology, head and neck disorders, internal medicine, plastic surgery, oncology, urology, and general surgery. Physicians throughout northwestern Ohio and southeastern Michigan often refer patients to Hayes Medical Center and to its various specialists.

The Center includes the following service departments: accounting, admissions, laboratory, medical records, human resources, and radiology. The staff includes doctors, nurses, administrative staff, and other employees.

Here is the organizational chart of Hayes Medical Center:

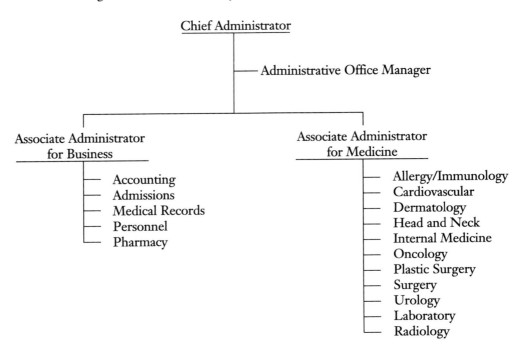

Chief Administrator
— Administrative Office Manager

Associate Administrator for Business
- Accounting
- Admissions
- Medical Records
- Personnel
- Pharmacy

Associate Administrator for Medicine
- Allergy/Immunology
- Cardiovascular
- Dermatology
- Head and Neck
- Internal Medicine
- Oncology
- Plastic Surgery
- Surgery
- Urology
- Laboratory
- Radiology

STAFF DIRECTORY

You will be communicating with many members of the staff and will need to recognize their names and titles. Refer to the Staff Directory at the back of this textbook for the correct spelling of names, office locations, and telephone numbers.

General Information

The following procedures have been developed for Hayes Medical Center and its staff. Some of these procedures may be updated periodically to meet the needs of patients and staff and to effectively use the equipment within the Center.

APPOINTMENTS

Patient appointments, including those patients referred to Hayes Medical Center, are scheduled with a physician in the appropriate medical specialty area. Every effort is made to schedule a day and time that is convenient for the patient.

CONFIDENTIALITY

Hayes Medical Center personnel often receive inquiries about a patient's physical condition. Information about a patient may be released only to the patient or, with the consent of a patient, to a member of the immediate family or a person who has power of attorney. In such cases, Hayes Medical Center personnel must recognize the family member. An individual who is designated in a legal document, e.g., a living will, a guardianship, or a power of attorney, may receive patient information if such papers are on file at the Center.

EMERGENCY CARE

Patients needing emergency care who are able to travel are referred to Emergency Admissions at Memorial Hospital. For patients with no transportation, an ambulance may be called (555-6000). Urgent life-threatening situations may require immediate attention by one of the Center's physicians.

LODGING AND DINING FACILITIES

Hayes Medical Center assists overnight patients and their families in securing lodging and dining facilities. The Owens Motel, located across the street from the Center, reserves a number of rooms and suites each day for patients and families. Full dining facilities are provided at the motel. A courtesy van is available for transportation to and from the Toledo Express Airport.

Patients can obtain additional information or make reservations by writing or calling the motel at 3234 Riverside Drive, Perrysburg, OH 43551-1002; 419-555-6211.

OFFICE HOURS

Hayes Medical Center is open Monday, Tuesday, Wednesday, and Friday from 8 a.m. to 12 noon and 1:30 to 5 p.m. On Thursday, the Center is open from 8 a.m. to 12 noon. An answering service receives all incoming calls and records messages when the office is closed. Doctors are on call on a rotating schedule during evenings and weekends.

PAYMENT FOR SERVICES

It is important for patients to know about our payment policy. Payment should be made immediately upon completion of an appointment. We accept cash, checks, Visa, or MasterCard for payment of fees.

For those patients who receive Medicare assistance or who have other appropriate insurance coverage, we will submit the insurance claims for them. The patients are responsible for costs not assumed by Medicare or their insurance carrier.

Supplies

Your textbook and your data disk contain documents and files that you will use while working at the Center.

TEXTBOOK

At the end of this Procedures Manual you will find model documents to help you correctly format various documents. The left margin of your textbook contains notes and reminders. Refer to them before you begin typing documents. They also contain helpful language arts tips and other information that you will find useful.

In the back of the textbook you will find staff and patient directories; a glossary of medicines and medical terminology; and a list of medical abbreviations. Use this information for reference throughout your work in the Center.

You will also find Job Profile, Medicines and Medical Terminology, and Technical Data Charts at the back of the textbook to help you keep track of your work in each unit and to record definitions and other technical data that you frequently type.

DATA DISK

Your data disk contains several files that you will need to use throughout your work at Hayes Medical Center. Before you use the data disk, make a backup copy. Use the backup copy for class, and keep the original in a safe place. Store your completed work on a blank disk to ensure that you don't run out of space on your data disk.

Formatting Guidelines

Hayes Medical Center has established guidelines that you should follow whenever you prepare documents for the Center. These guidelines are presented in alphabetical order, so you may want to read through them before you begin preparing any documents. Refer to these guidelines as often as necessary during your work at the Center.

Complimentary Closing. Use the closing *Sincerely yours,* in all correspondence.

Copy Notation. Copies of patient-related reports and letters should be sent to referring physicians. Type the copy notation (*c:*) on the line below the reference initials. Press the tab key before typing the name.

Date of Birth. Consultation letters require a date of birth (**DOB**). Type **DOB:** and the actual date in bold on the line below the subject line. The date should be typed in the following format: mm/dd/yy; for example, 5/15/45.

Dates. When you must supply a date, type the current date and year. If you insert the date automatically, be sure that it will not be changed if you open the document again at a later time. In instances where you must calculate dates (e.g., two weeks from today), use a current calendar to determine the exact dates. For example, if in a letter dated March 17, 2000, you must provide the date of the patient's examination two weeks ago, you would type *March 3, 2000.*

Distribution Lists. When a memo is being sent to more than three people, use a distribution list. After the heading, *MEMO TO:*, type the words, *See Distribution Below*. Then, two lines after the last line of the memo, type *Distribution:* in italic. Press Enter two times and type the list of names in alphabetical order, aligned at the left margin.

Document Codes. Type a document code on every document so that you can easily identify printed copies. The document code should be the file name under which you save your document. Use the job number as the file name (for example, *job09*). Using a zero before single digit numbers will ensure that your saved documents are in sequential order.

If a document requires reference initials, type your initials followed by a diagonal (/) and the document code (*urs/job12*). If there are no reference initials, type the document code at the left margin, 2 lines below the last line of text.

Enclosure Notations. Type an enclosure or attachment notation on the next line following the reference initials.

File Names. Save each production job onto a data disk. Unless otherwise directed, use the document code as the file name (for example, *job01, job02*, etc.). Adding a zero before a single-digit number will ensure that the jobs are in sequential order on your disk.

Font. Use Times New Roman 12 pt for all documents unless otherwise noted.

Generic or Chemical Names. Do not capitalize generic or chemical names of drugs or medications. Do capitalize trade names or brand names of medications which contain those chemicals or drugs (e.g., *acetaminophen, Tylenol Cold & Flu, menthol, Mentholatum Rub*).

When generic or chemical names are typed in a list, such as in a medical report, capitalize the first word. Type any drug or medication to which a patient is allergic in all capital letters and bold.

Letters. All correspondence for Hayes Medical Center and the individual specialty units should be typed in block format, with standard punctuation, on the correct letterhead.

Margins. Use 1-inch top, bottom, and side margins for all documents unless otherwise noted. There may be instances where the bottom margin is greater than 1 inch. For example, if the closing lines of a letter carry over to a second page, adjust the page break on the first page so at least two lines of text appear at the top of the second page.

Numbered or Bulleted Lists. Leave a blank line between each numbered or bulleted item in a list.

Page Numbers. Number continuation pages of all multipage documents.

In letters and memos, create a header for continuation pages that includes the addressee's name, the page number, and the date in block format. Refer to the Model Documents section for an illustration.

In all other medical documents, create a footer that contains a 1-row table with the name of the report, the patient's name, the date, and the page numbers displayed as *Page x of x.*

Physician Names. In medical documents, letters, and forms, type the full name of the physician or staff member followed by his or her degree.

Thomas Eadie, M.D.

Leslie A. Scott
Audiologist

In salutations of letters and consultation reports, use staff members' professional titles and last names (e.g., *Dear Dr. Eadie:*; *Dear Ms. Scott:*).

In closing lines, type the physician's name and title 4 lines below the last line of text or complimentary closing, if there is one. Depending on the kind of report, the physician's name and title may begin at the center or 1 inch from the left margin.

Printing. Print one copy of each completed document unless otherwise instructed.

Proofreading. Proofread all of your documents. This is essential even if you use a spelling checker. For example, a spelling checker cannot distinguish between *word* and *work* or *Osborne* and *Osborn.*

RE:. Use *RE:* for the subject line in all patient-related correspondence. Type the letters followed by a colon in all capital letters and bold, and the patient's name in initial capital letters (no bold).

In all consultation letters, type the entire subject line in bold followed by the patient's date of birth on the next line, also in bold.

Reference Initials. Type your initials in lowercase letters 2 lines below the writer's name and title on all letters and medical reports. Do not type initials on medical and administrative forms.

Reports. For standard reports (non-medical and those not on letterhead), leave an approximate 2-inch top margin. On all other reports, type the title a double space below the unit name or the letterhead. Center and type all report titles in all caps, bold, and underlined.

Spelling and Typographical Errors. Use the spelling feature of your software to check your documents for spelling and typographical errors. However, you will still need to proofread your documents.

Many medical terms are not included in spelling checker dictionaries. Therefore, your instructor may ask you to add the medical terms at the beginning of each unit to a supplementary dictionary. If so, be sure to use the supplemental dictionary to check the spelling in your documents.

Subject Line. Type a subject line in all patient-related medical letters 2 lines below the salutation. Type *RE:* in all capital letters and bold, and the patient's name in initial capital letters (no bold).

In a consultation report or consultation letter, type the entire subject line in bold followed by the patient's date of birth (also in bold) on the next line.

Technical Data. Type all significant numbers and statistics in figures and symbols, not in words, to avoid possible misreading of the data (for example, *78-year-old female; Capoten 25 mg 3 per day; respirations were 18; check the patient again in 5 weeks; 85% of the maximum predicted heart rate*). However, numbers at the beginning of sentences should be typed in words.

Widow/Orphan Protection. Turn on widow/orphan protection at the beginning of all multipage documents to ensure that a page does not end with a single line that begins a paragraph and does not begin with a single line that ends a paragraph. If necessary, insert a hard page break to make any adjustments.

Word Division Rules

Follow these general rules when processing medical documents:

- Do not divide a proper noun except at the hyphen if it is a compound word (e.g., *Neo-Synephrine*).
- Divide compound words either at the hyphen (*symptom-free*) or where two words join to make a solid compound (*aero-odontalgia*, not *aero-odon-talgia*).
- Do not split dates between lines; however, the year, if written in full, may be carried to the next line.
- If a name contains a professional title (*Dr. Daniel Barnett*), do not split it between lines. However, if it also contains a middle initial, you may split it after the initial.

Spacing With Punctuation and Symbols

Type punctuation marks and symbols with spaces before and after as follows:

Ampersand. One space before and after unless otherwise noted.

Closing Quotation Mark. (a) Typed after a period or comma and before a colon or semicolon. (b) Typed after a question mark or exclamation mark if the quoted material is a question or an exclamation; otherwise, typed before the question mark or exclamation point.

Colon. One space after.

Comma. One space after.

Exclamation Point. One space after.

Period. One space after a period at the end of a sentence; one space after the period following initials or an abbreviation (*Dr. K. Smith*); no space after each internal period in a closed abbreviation (*p.m. or b.i.d*).

Question Mark. One space after.

Semicolon. One space after.

ZIP Code. One space before. Nine-digit ZIP Codes are typed with no internal spaces (*43081-1096*).

Symbols

$=$	(equal)	One space before and after.
$\times$	(times)	One space before and after.
$+$	(plus)	No space between the symbol and the measurement, reading, and so on ($+2$, A+). If used in a formula, one space before and after.
%	(percent)	No space before and one space after (except at the end of a sentence when it is followed by punctuation).
$>$	(greater than)	One space before and after.
$<$	(less than)	One space before and after.
°	(degree)	No space before and one space after (except at the end of a sentence when it is followed by punctuation).

Proofreaders' Marks

Proofreaders' Mark		Draft	Final Copy
SS	single space	SS ⌜first line ⌞second line	first line second line
ds	double space	ds ⌜first line ⌞second line	first line second line
∧ or ∨	insert punctuation	Ruths 6 -month rash	Ruth's 6-month rash
new / old	change word	a left femoral _(right)_	a right femoral
ᵔ	delete and close up	aero-biology	aerobiology
/	lowercase	our Director	our director
⌇⌇⌇⌇	type in bold	IMPRESSION	**IMPRESSION**
——	type in italic	the Gazette	the _Gazette_
◯	spell out	(Jan. 9)	January 9
—— u/s	underline	for 32 hours u/s	for 32 hours
⊐	move right	⊐ On the first	On the first
⊏	move left	⊏ Last month	Last month
◠	omit space	finger tip	fingertip
∽	transpose	the ⌐fundi optic⌐	the optic fundi
∧	insert word(s)	of ∧coma _(diabetic)_	of diabetic coma
☰	capitalize	Freehoffer clinic	Freehoffer Clinic
ℓ	delete	is not the toe	is the toe
↗	move as shown	dressing wrapped (was) transferred to	dressing was wrapped transferred to
¶	paragraph	symptoms. ¶The heart	symptoms. The heart
#⁄∧	insert space	of∧the lower #	of the lower
⊙	make a period	per liter⊙	per liter.
·····	do not change	his right knee	his right knee
# ⟩	insert line	# ⟩ Name Date	Name Date

Formats

Consultation Letter, page 1

HAYES MEDICAL CENTER
3231 Riverside Drive
Perrysburg, OH 43551-1001
Phone 419-555-7800   Fax 419-555-7890
Excellence in Medical Service for Over 50 Years

2 ↓   INTERNAL MEDICINE UNIT   ↓ 2

Current Date
↓ 4

Dominic Marini, M.D.
Northside Internal Medicine
73 Snow Road, Suite 641
Parma, OH 44129   ↓ 2

Dear Dr. Marini: ↓ 2

RE: Crystal J. Ford
DOB: 11/23/69   ↓ 2

Crystal J. Ford is a 31-year-old, right-handed female who now has resolving what appears to be right posterior interosseous nerve entrapment. Initially, there had been consideration of EMG study of the right upper extremity. Given her symptomatic improvement with cessation of certain activities, this is deferred.   ↓ 2

She now comes in with a new complaint related to doing some pull climbing at work. This involves dysesthesia in a right median distribution as well as in a left ulnar distribution. Relevant NCV studies were performed. This includes a right median motor and sensory conduction, right ulnar sensory action potential, left median sensory action potential, and left ulnar motor and sensory conductions. Orthodromic stimulation technique was used to elicit sensory action potentials with latency measurements to peak.

The right median nerve shows a distal motor latency of 2.6 msec at a distance of 6 cm with forearm segmental conduction velocity of 57.4 msec with F wave occurring at 25.6 msec. Amplitude was 27.7 mv with stimulation at the wrist and 26.9 mv with stimulation at the elbow. The right median sensory action potential showed a latency of 3.0 msec at a distance of 12 cm with mild temporal dispersion and an amplitude of 14.8 µV. The right median palm-to-wrist segmental conduction velocity was 34.1 msec at the lower limits of normal with a latency of 1.76 msec and amplitude of 102 µV. The right ulnar sensory action potential showed a latency of 2.3 msec at a distance of 10 cm with an amplitude of 14 µV.

The left median sensory action potential showed a latency of 2.7 msec at a distance of 12 cm with an amplitude of 43.8 µV. The left ulnar distal motor latency was 3.0 msec at a distance of 6 cm with forearm segmental conduction velocity of 61.2 msec, velocity across the ulnar groove of

Consultation Letter, page 1

Consultation Letter, page 2

Dominic Marini, M.D.
Page 2
Current Date

75 msec with amplitudes of 13.5 mv with stimulation at the wrist, 15.7 mv with stimulation below the ulnar groove, and 15.8 mv above the ulnar groove with F wave occurring at 26.8 msec. The left ulnar sensory action potential showed a latency of 2.3 msec at a distance of 10 cm with amplitude of 19.1 µV.

IMPRESSION: NCV studies of the arms disclosed the following:

1. There is evidence for a very minimal carpal tunnel entrapment of the right median nerve, given a high normal sensory action potential latency on the right side compared with the left, with a definite asymmetry in amplitude of the sensory action potential, with the right side being lower than the left by a considerable margin. There are no other abnormalities of motor conduction, and these findings are emphasized to be minimal.

2. There is no electrodiagnostic evidence for tardy ulnar palsy on the left although irritation of the root with frank electrodiagnostic change by standard NCV criteria cannot be excluded.   ↓ 2

3. The normalcy of the right ulnar and left median sensory action potentials militates against a diffuse peripheral neuropathy. F waves are normal for the right median and left ulnar nerves as well.   ↓ 2

Sincerely yours,   ↓ 4

Michael McGinty, M.D.   ↓ 2

urs/jobxx

Consultation Letter, page 2

Memo With Distribution List

HAYES MEDICAL CENTER
3231 Riverside Drive
Perrysburg, OH 43551-1001
Phone 419-555-7800   Fax 419-555-7890
Excellence in Medical Service for Over 50 Years

ADMISSIONS

MEMO TO: See Distribution Below   ↓ 2

FROM: Connie Lawlor, Head of Admissions   ↓ 2

DATE: Current Date   ↓ 2

SUBJECT: New Patient Information Form   ↓ 2

Attached is a draft of the New Patient Information Form I have developed. Shirley Martek has worked with me in developing the revised form. We think this form is a great improvement over the current admission form.

Please suggest other data that you feel might be useful on the form. Send any corrections, additions, or changes to me by the end of next week.

Thank you for your input.   ↓ 2

Attachment
urs/jobxx   ↓ 2

Distribution: ↓ 2

Georgia Hart, Department Head
Diane Oster, Office Assistant
Neil Roberts, M.D.
Marge Ryan, Office Assistant
Leslie Scott, Audiologist
Michael Tridon, Office Assistant

Memo With Distribution List

Authorization for Release

HAYES MEDICAL CENTER
3231 Riverside Drive
Perrysburg, OH 43551-1001
Phone 419-555-7800   Fax 419-555-7890
Excellence in Medical Service for Over 50 Years

AUTHORIZATION FOR RELEASE OF MEDICAL INFORMATION

In an effort to avoid duplication, and thereby help control costs, I hereby authorize and request

_____
Physician or Medical Group

to release the following information contained in my records, including information about Human Immune Deficiency Virus Positivity (HIV+), Acquired Immune Deficiency Syndrome (AIDS), and AIDS-Related Complex (ARC), as defined by the Ohio Department of Public Health.

Patient Name _____   Date of Birth _____

_____ History and Physical	_____ X-ray/MRI Report
_____ Laboratory Reports	_____ Surgery Report
_____ Pathology Reports	_____ Progress Report
_____ Audiology Reports	_____ All Medical Records
_____ Discharge Summary	_____ Treatment Summary
_____ Other	

To: _____
_____
_____
_____

I understand that I may revoke this authorization at any time and that it automatically expires once the purpose for which it was intended is accomplished. My signature means that I have read this form and/or have had it read to me and explained in language that I can understand.

_____   _____
Signature of Patient, Parent, or Guardian   Today's Date

job17

Authorization for Release

Return Visit Report, page 1

HAYES MEDICAL CENTER
3231 Riverside Drive
Perrysburg, OH 43551-1001

Phone 419-555-7800   Fax 419-555-7890
Excellence in Medical Service for Over 50 Years

CARDIOVASCULAR MEDICINE UNIT

RETURN VISIT

Name	Weight	B.P.
Stanley Stark	175 lb	140/78
Date	H.R.	
Correct Date	72	

Current Meds

Procardia XL 60 mg q.i.d.	Trental
Digoxin 0.125 mg q.i.d.	Zantac
Transderm-Nitro	Aspirin grains 5 q.i.d.

The patient was seen to review the results of the stress MUGA test performed at Memorial Hospital on December 7, 1997. The patient reached an exertional level of 5 MET. and 60% of maximum predicted heart rate without symptoms of chest discomfort. There were nondiagnostic changes on EKG. The MUGA scan demonstrated resting left ventricular ejection fraction of 40% with decrease during exercise to 31%.

The patient is known to have coronary artery disease with the most recent cardiac catheterization in July 1997, showing total occlusion of the proximal circumflex artery with collateral filling in the distal vessel, 80% stenosis of the midanterior descending artery, and mild disease within the right coronary artery. The previous cardiac catheterization in January 1995 had demonstrated total occlusion of the proximal anterior descending artery with collateral filling in the distal vessel, and thus the lesion identified in July 1997 represented recanalization of an occluded vessel. The patient had undergone coronary angioplasty of 80% lesion in the proximal circumflex artery in January 1995, which then progressed to full occlusion at the time of cardiac catheterization in July 1997. The previous exercise MUGA test in October 1995 had also demonstrated an exertional level of 5 MET. with development of symptoms of chest discomfort. At that time, the resting left ventricular ejection fraction was only 30% and the postexercise ejection fraction was identical to the current study at 31%.

In August 1994 the patient had been admitted to Memorial Hospital with onset of atrial fibrillation. The rhythm converted to sinus following institution of Digoxin. An acute myocardial infarction was excluded during that admission, and a subsequent exercise thallium test performed on August 7, 1994, at Memorial Hospital had demonstrated an exertional level of 5.5 MET. without symptoms of chest pain or definite EKG evidence of myocardial ischemia. The

RETURN VISIT	Stanley Stark	Current Date	Page 1 of 2

Return Visit Report, page 2

simultaneous thallium scan at that time demonstrated old infarction without definite evidence of exercise-induced ischemia.

In recent months the patient has continued to have occasional symptoms of exertional chest pain, but no symptoms of chest pain at rest, orthopnea, or PND. The patient has noted some improvement in symptoms of dyspnea with exertion in recent months.

It was discussed with the patient that in light of the stability of symptoms, findings on exercise thallium test at Memorial Hospital in August 1994, and unchanged postexercise left ventricular ejection fraction on the current exercise MUGA test compared to the previous study in 1997, there appears to be no definite evidence of progression of coronary disease. The current medications will be continued. The plan will be to continue to perform periodic repeat exercise tests to evaluate for possible evidence of progression of coronary disease. It was also discussed with the patient that if he should have a change in symptoms of exertional chest pain or dyspnea, then consideration will be given for repeat cardiac catheterization to determine if there has been a change in coronary anatomy compared to the previous cardiac catheterization in 1997. The patient will be seen in follow-up by Dr. Eadie and will be seen again in this office for the periodic repeat cardiac evaluation or PRN.

center   Jeffrey Szabo, M.D.

urs/job31
c: Daniel Barnett, M.D.

RETURN VISIT	Stanley Stark	Current Date	Page 2 of 2

Patient Data File 1

HAYES MEDICAL CENTER
3231 Riverside Drive
Perrysburg, OH 43551-1001

Phone 419-555-7800   Fax 419-555-7890
Excellence in Medical Service for Over 50 Years

PLASTIC SURGERY UNIT

PATIENT DATA FILE

DATE: Current Date

PATIENT'S NAME: William Q. Otto

DOB: 5/4/33

PHYSICIAN: Janice S. Karns, M.D.

DATE OF EXAM: April 3, {year}

CHIEF COMPLAINT: Bleeding lesion of the right temple.

CONSULTATION: Mr. Otto is a 66-year-old male who was referred by his family physician because of a lesion that has been bleeding the last several months. The patient indicated that he has had this small lesion on his right temple for about a year, but he thought very little of it. It has grown in size, now measuring almost 1 cm in diameter. In the past few months, every time he washes and dries his face, blood appears on the towel. He occasionally has a burning sensation.

His past medical history is significant in that he had a myocardial infarct in the past and also has hypertension. He is on Procardia and, on occasion, takes nitroglycerin for chest pain. He is allergic to **ERYTHROMYCIN.**

Physical examination shows an umbilicated lesion on the right temple that on vigorous touching bleeds slightly. The borders are raised.

I explained to Mr. Otto that his lesion has the clinical appearance of a basal cell carcinoma. I also explained to him that skin cancer is locally invasive and that it does not usually metastasize. I advised an excision to be done under local anesthesia. The procedure and what to expect were explained to him. His questions were answered and we agreed to perform the procedure.

Patrick Nehlson, M.D.

urs/jobxx

PATIENT DATA FILE	William Q. Otto	April 3, {year}	Page 1 of 1

Patient Data File 2

HAYES MEDICAL CENTER
3231 Riverside Drive
Perrysburg, OH 43551-1001

Phone 419-555-7800   Fax 419-555-7890
Excellence in Medical Service for Over 50 Years

PLASTIC SURGERY UNIT

PATIENT DATA FILE

DATE: Current Date

PATIENT'S NAME: William Q. Otto

DOB: 5/4/33

PHYSICIAN: Janice S. Karns, M.D.

DATE OF EXAM: April 23, {year}

The patient had his operation a week ago. His incision is healing very nicely. I removed the sutures today and discussed his pathology report with him, which did show a basal cell carcinoma. It has been completely excised, and nothing more needs to be done. I also have discussed with him avoiding the sun, wearing a hat in summer, and using sunscreen.

Patrick Nehlson, M.D.

urs/jobxx

PATIENT DATA FILE	William Q. Otto	April 23, {year}	Page 1 of 1

Operative Consent, page 1

HAYES MEDICAL CENTER
3231 Riverside Drive
Perrysburg, OH 43551-1001
Phone 419-555-7800   Fax 419-555-7890
Excellence in Medical Service for Over 50 Years

OPERATIVE CONSENT

This is an agreement between Dr. Janice Karns and myself, William Q. Otto, summarizing our discussion and knowledge of the conditions under which we consent to treat a bleeding lesion of the right temple scheduled for (supply date).

I understand that Dr. Janice Karns will use his/her best skill and judgment to attain the desired results, but that he/she cannot and does not guarantee such results. I further understand that the physician's prediction of the length of time involved, the manner of recovery, and possible complications or adverse results is based upon the average response in similar cases. I understand that my response may be different from the usual response.

I understand that Dr. Janice Karns will choose the best results achievable from a physical and/or artistic viewpoint. I promise to cooperate and consent to any method of treatment that seems to have the best chance for success.

I understand that the fee of $800 agreed upon for the operation covers the surgery and the usual postoperative care rendered by Dr. Janice Karns and staff at his/her office and hospital. Regular hospital expenses, laboratory fees, etc., are not included.

I authorize Dr. Janice Karns and such assistants, photographers, and technicians as he/she may engage for this purpose, to take photographs of me as he/she directs before, during, and after the operation. I also authorize such photographs to be published in professional journals and medical books or to be used for any purpose that my physician deems necessary in the interest of medical education, knowledge, or research. Further, I give permission for the modification and/or

(over)

Operative Consent, page 1

Operative Consent, page 2

publication of these photographs and/or information relating to my case. If the photographs concerning my case are published, it is specifically understood that I will not be identified by name.

_____   _____
Patient's Signature   Date

_____   _____
Parent's or Guardian's Signature   Witness's Signature

_____   _____
Surgeon's Signature   Date

jobxx

Operative Consent, page 2

Vaccine Consent, page 1

HAYES MEDICAL CENTER
3231 Riverside Drive
Perrysburg, OH 43551-1001
Phone 419-555-7800   Fax 419-555-7890
Excellence in Medical Service for Over 50 Years

ALLERGY/IMMUNOLOGY UNIT

INFLUENZA (FLU) VACCINE
CONSENT FORM

THE FLU: Influenza (flu) is a respiratory infection caused by viruses. When people get the flu, they may have symptoms of fever, chills, headache, dry cough, or muscle aches. Illness may last several days or a week or more, and complete recovery is usual. However, complications could lead to pneumonia or death.

It is not possible to estimate the risk of a person getting the flu this year. Nonetheless, for the elderly and for people with asthma, diabetes, or heart, lung, or kidney diseases, flu may be especially serious.

THE VACCINE: An injection of flu vaccine will not give you flu because the vaccine is made from killed viruses. The vaccine is developed from viruses selected by the Office of Biologics, the Food and Drug Administration, and the Public Health Service.

RISKS AND POSSIBLE REACTIONS: The reactions to influenza vaccine are generally mild in adults and occur at low frequency. These reactions consist of tenderness at the injection site, fever, chills, headaches, or muscular aches. These symptoms can last up to 48 hours.

A small number of people who received the 1976 swine flu vaccine suffered a paralysis called Guillain-Barré Syndrome (GBS). GBS is typically characterized by a paralysis that begins in the hands or feet and then moves up the arms or legs or both. GBS is usually self-limiting and most persons with GBS recover without permanent weakness. However, in approximately 5 percent of the cases, a permanent or even fatal form of paralysis may occur. In 1976 GBS appeared with excess frequency among people who had received the 1976 swine flu vaccine. For the 10 weeks following vaccination, the risk of GBS was found to be approximately 10 cases for every 1 million people vaccinated. This represents a risk 5 to 6 times higher than unvaccinated people would face. Younger persons (under 25 years of age) had a lower risk than others and also had a lower fatality rate.

Data on the occurrence of GBS have been collected during 3 influenza seasons since the surveillance began in 1978. These data suggest that, in contrast to the 1976 situation, the risk of GBS in recipients of influenza vaccine was not significantly higher than that in nonrecipients. Nonetheless, persons who receive influenza vaccine should be aware of this possible risk as compared with the risk of influenza and its complications.

SPECIAL PRECAUTIONS: Children under 3 years of age have some increased risk of febrile convulsions. Pregnant women should consult with their obstetricians before receiving the vaccine.

People who are allergic to eggs or egg products should not receive this vaccine without informing us of such allergies, which may require testing for tolerance to the vaccine before it is administered.

(over)

Vaccine Consent, page 1

Vaccine Consent, page 2

People with fever should not receive this vaccine. People who have received another type of vaccine within the past 14 days should see their personal physicians before receiving this vaccine.

If you have a reaction to the injection, contact a physician immediately. Please let us know if you have any questions before you sign this form.

CONSENT: I have read the above information and have had an opportunity to ask questions. I understand the benefits and risks of flu vaccination as described herein. I request that the vaccine be given to me or to the person named below for whom I am authorized to sign.

Information Concerning Person to Receive Influenza Vaccine

_____   _____   _____
Full Name (Please Print)   Date of Birth   Age

_____ _____ _____ _____
Address   City   State   ZIP

_____
Signature of Person to Receive Vaccine (or Parent or Guardian)

_____   _____
Witness   Date

jobxxx

Vaccine Consent, page 2

Memorial Hospital Operative Report, page 1

MEMORIAL HOSPITAL
936 West Broadway
Maumee, OH 43537-1220

MEDICAL RECORDS

Name of Patient	Physician	Room No.	History No.
Pamela C. Haggerty	Mildred Phelps, M.D.	345	10060

SURGERY UNIT

OPERATIVE REPORT

ADMITTED: Current Date

DISCHARGED:

DICTATED: Current Date

OPERATION: Laparoscopic cholecystectomy

PREOP DIAGNOSIS: Cholelithiasis

POSTOP DIAGNOSIS: Same

ANESTHESIA: General endotracheal

PROCEDURE: The patient was brought into the operating room and placed on the table in a supine position. After induction of general endotracheal anesthesia, a Foley catheter was placed and the abdomen prepped and draped sterilely.

The patient was placed in Trendelenburg's position. A small incision was made at the umbilicus. The abdominal wall was grasped and elevated with sharp towel clips. A Veress needle was passed into the abdomen. Clear intraperitoneal position was confirmed by aspiration and inflow of saline with the drop test. The abdomen was inflated with CO2. Low insufflation pressures were present. When satisfactory pneumoperitoneum was achieved, the Veress needle was removed and a 10 mm trocar passed at the umbilical site.

Intraperitoneal position was confirmed with the video laparoscope. No evidence of bowel injury or bleeding was present. The upper abdomen was then visualized and the patient was placed in reverse Trendelenburg's position. Two 5 mm trocars were passed in the right subcostal area. These sites were passed under direct vision. The 5 mm sites were used for grasping forceps which manipulated and retracted the gallbladder. A 10 mm trocar was passed in the upper midline position. This site was also passed under direct vision. The 10 mm site was used for dissection, clip application, electrocautery, etc. The fundus of the gallbladder was then grasped and elevated towards the right shoulder. The infundibular region was also grasped and placed on traction. Calot's triangle was dissected bluntly. The fibroperitoneal tissue in this area was spread and

OPERATIVE REPORT	Pamela C. Haggerty	Current Date	Page 1 of 2

Memorial Hospital Operative Report, page 2

stripped towards the common duct. Using this technique, the cystic duct and artery were clearly identified. These structures were followed onto the gallbladder. The common duct was visualized through the peritoneum and was well away from the area of dissection. The cystic duct and artery were then controlled with clips and divided. The posterior vascular branch was also clipped and divided. The gallbladder was freed from its bed using blunt technique and the electrocautery unit. Prior to dividing the last attachments to the gallbladder, the intrahepatic region was irrigated and examined. No active bleeding or other abnormalities were present. The final attachments to the gallbladder were divided and the gallbladder removed through the upper 10 mm trocar site. The trocar replaced, and the perihepatic region again irrigated and examined. No active bleeding or other abnormalities were present. The pneumoperitoneum was evacuated and the trocar removed. The skin was then closed with 3-0 Vicryl subcuticular sutures. Steri-Strips and dressing were applied and the patient was taken to the recovery room in stable condition.

Mildred Phelps, M.D.

urs/jobxx

OPERATIVE REPORT	Pamela C. Haggerty	Current Date	Page 2 of 2

Echocardiogram Report, page 1

HAYES MEDICAL CENTER
3231 Riverside Drive
Perrysburg, OH 43551-1001

Phone 419-555-7800   Fax 419-555-7890

Excellence in Medical Service for Over 50 Years

CARDIOVASCULAR MEDICINE UNIT

ECHOCARDIOGRAM REPORT

DATE: Current Date

PATIENT NAME: Hyung Il Lee

REFERRING PHYSICIAN: Justine Lawrence, M.D.

DATE OF TEST: Current

HISTORY AND INDICATION FOR TESTING: This is a male who was seen in the office with an episode that sounded like a TIA. Previous 2-D echo Dopplers have revealed only mild thickening of the aortic valve.

M-MODE INTERPRETATION: This is a technically difficult study. The aortic valve is visualized and appears to be thickened but with adequate opening to 2.2 cm. The aortic root is normal in dimension at 3.2 cm. The left atrium measures 3.7 cm. The mitral valve motion appeared grossly normal with no evident prolapse. There is a normal appearing E point to septal separation. The left ventricle appeared mildly enlarged, but this enlargement may be due to orientation with the measurement in the minor diameter of 6.3 cm; contractility was good with a fractional shortening of 44%. There was no pericardial effusion.

2-D EXAMINATION: This is a technically difficult study. The patient's heart seems to lie in a longitudinal manner with the ventricles appearing almost vertical in the subcostal view. The apical views were obtained near the parasternal border with the patient lying fully in the left lateral decubitus position. The aortic valve in the long-axis and short-axis view appears thickened but opens normally. The mitral and tricuspid valves appear normal. The pulmonic valve is not well visualized. The cardiac chambers overall appear normal in size. The left ventricle exhibited normal contractility. There was no detectable apical thrombus. There is no pericardial effusion.

DOPPLER INTERPRETATION: Pulsed- and continuous-wave Doppler was performed. There was no detectable aortic regurgitation. Trace mitral insufficiency was present.

FINAL COMMENTS:

1.   Technically difficult but adequate study based on configuration of the patient's heart.

ECHOCARDIOGRAM REPORT	Hyung Il Lee	Current Date	Page 1 of 2

Echocardiogram Report, page 2

2.   Thickened aortic valve without regurgitation or stenosis.

3.   Trace mitral insufficiency.

4.   Normal cardiac chambers and left ventricular function.

5.   No detectable ventricular thrombus.

The only potential, although unlikely, source of cardiac emboli would be the thickened aortic valve which appears unchanged from a previous study.

Jason Karns, M.D.

urs/jobxx
c: Justine Lawrence, M.D.

ECHOCARDIOGRAM REPORT	Hyung Il Lee	Current Date	Page 2 of 2

Patient Information Form, page 1

HAYES MEDICAL CENTER   PATIENT INFORMATION
3231 Riverside Drive
Perrysburg, OH 43551-1001
419-555-7800

PLEASE PRINT YOUR ANSWERS. RETURN THIS FORM TO THE RECEPTIONIST.

PATIENT'S NAME _____
               Last   First   Initial

STREET ADDRES _____

CITY _____ STATE _____ ZIP _____

HOME PHONE _____ WORK PHONE _____ ____

BIRTH DATE _____ AGE _____ SEX _____ SS NO. _____

MARITAL STATUS: SINGLE _____   MARRIED _____   WIDOWED _____   DIVORCED _____

FAMILY DOCTOR AND ADDRESS _____

_____

REFERRAL SOURCE _____

YOUR EMPLOYER _____

EMPLOYER'S ADDRESS _____

IF YOU ARE A MINOR, PLEASE PROVIDE THE FOLLOWING INFORMATION:

FATHER'S NAME _____

ADDRESS _____

FATHER'S EMPLOYER _____

EMPLOYER'S ADDRESS _____

MOTHER'S NAME _____

ADDRESS _____

MOTHER'S EMPLOYER _____

EMPLOYER'S ADDRESS _____

ARE YOU BEING SEEN FOR A WORK-RELATED INJURY?   YES _____ NO _____

ARE YOU BEING SEEN FOR AN AUTO-RELATED INJURY?   YES _____ NO _____

(over)

Patient Information Form, page 1

Patient Information Form, page 2

INSURANCE INFORMATION

PRIMARY INSURANCE NAME _____

POLICY NO. _____ GROUP NO. _____

POLICYHOLDER'S NAME _____

INSURANCE COMPANY'S ADDRESS _____

_____

SECONDARY INSURANCE NAME _____

POLICY NO. _____ GROUP NO. _____

POLICYHOLDER'S NAME _____

INSURANCE COMPANY'S ADDRESS _____

_____

WE SUBMIT INSURANCE CLAIMS FOR OUR PATIENTS.

HOW WILL YOU PAY FOR YOUR OFFICE VISIT TODAY?

CASH _____   CHECK _____   VISA® _____   MASTERCARD® _____

I HEREBY AUTHORIZE RELEASE OF INFORMATION NECESSARY TO FILE A CLAIM WITH MY INSURANCE COMPANY AND TO ASSIGN BENEFITS OTHERWISE PAYABLE TO ME TO THE PHYSICIAN OR THE CENTER AS INDICATED ON THE CLAIM. A COPY OF THE SIGNATURE IS AS VALID AS THE ORIGINAL.

SIGNATURE OF PATIENT OR RESPONSIBLE PARTY

_____

DATE _____

jobx-xx

Patient Information Form, page 2

HMC Radiology Report, page 1

HAYES MEDICAL CENTER
3231 Riverside Drive
Perrysburg, OH 43551-1001
Phone 419-555-7800   Fax 419-555-7890
Excellence in Medical Service for Over 50 Years

RADIOLOGY DEPARTMENT

RADIOLOGY REPORT

DATE: Current Date

PATIENT NAME: Kenneth David

DOB: 10/11/50

REFERRING PHYSICIAN: Nancy Veenstra, M.D.

DATE OF EXAM: Current Date

X RAY NO.: 199232

EXAMINATION: Lumbar Spine, Pelvis

LUMBAR SPINE: Examination of the lumbar spine in 5 views reveals a dextrorotoscoliosis. Degenerative changes are present in the spine. The apparent narrowing at L4-5 interspace may, in part, be related to projection. I believe this is most likely a true finding, however. A calcification in the right upper quadrant is noted. A gallstone is not excluded. Ultrasound of the gallbladder may aid. The pedicle, dorsal, and transverse processes are intact. No fracture is seen. No spondylolysis or spondylolisthesis is noted. Calcifications overlying the upper and lower portions of the right kidney are noted incidentally. On the lateral view, however, calcification is fairly far anteriorly. I doubt that this condition is due solely to calcification within the kidney. Ultrasound also would aid in evaluation of possible renal lithiasis.

IMPRESSION: Degenerative changes with dextrorotoscoliosis. Narrow L4-5 interspace. Possible gallstone; ultrasound may aid.

PELVIS: Examination of the pelvis in single AP view reveals degenerative changes and scoliosis in the low lumbar spine. The soft tissues are prominent. The pelvis appears intact. No fracture is seen. The hip joint spaces are unremarkable.

RADIOLOGY REPORT	Kenneth David	Current Date	Page 1 of 2

HMC Radiology Report, page 1

HMC Radiology Report, page 2

IMPRESSION: Essentially normal pelvis.

John P. Boland, M.D.
Radiologist

urs/jobxx

RADIOLOGY REPORT	Kenneth David	Current Date	Page 2 of 2

HMC Radiology Report, page 2

MH Radiology Report, page 1

MEMORIAL HOSPITAL   DEPARTMENT OF RADIOLOGY
936 West Broadway
Maumee, OH 43537-1220

Name of Patient		Sex	DOB	Medical Record No.
Marilyn D. Lopez		F	4/21/30	678459
Ordering Physician		Physician		
Shan Chung, M.D.		Donald Lincoln, M.D.		
Billing Code	Billing No.	Exam Date		Exam No.
70486	S14399802	*(Yesterday)*		2351

DESCRIPTION: CT OF PARANASAL SINUSES

INDICATION: Ethmoid sinusitis.

CT SCAN OF BRAIN: CT examination of the paranasal sinuses was performed utilizing contiguous 3-mm images in their coronal plane. This was performed without intravenous contrast.

There was marked asymmetry of the nasal turbinates with deviation of the nasal septum to the left side. An air fluid level was present in the dependent portion of the right maxillary sinus. Also noted were several soft-tissue densities along the roof, floor, and lateral walls of the maxillary sinus, which would suggest the presence of multiple polyps or retention cysts. There was mucosal thickening along the medial aspect of the left maxillary sinus. Patchy ethmoid air-cell consolidation was detected. The left osteomeatal unit was not well defined, suggesting occlusion. The right osteomeatal unit was better defined; however, this also appeared narrowed. The sphenoid sinus appeared unremarkable. There was very minimal mucosal thickening of the right frontal sinus.

Coronal images of the sinuses were obtained and supplemented with axial images. No contrast was administered. The osteomeatal unit was not well defined in this patient. There appeared to be a small polyp or retention cyst arising in the infrabital portion of the right maxillary sinus. Sinuses otherwise were well aerated, with no mucosal abnormality or bony changes being identified.

The superior aspect of the medial walls of the maxillary sinuses was not well defined. This raised the question of previous surgery, although we were not given a history of previous surgical intervention. Asymmetry and fullness of the turbinates suggested mucosal edema.

IMPRESSION:

1. EVIDENCE OF MUCOSAL THICKENING INVOLVING THE MAXILLARY, ETHMOID, AND FRONTAL SINUSES. THERE WAS ALSO SUGGESTION FOR MULTIPLE POLYPS OR RETENTION CYSTS WITHIN THE RIGHT MAXILLARY SINUS.

RADIOLOGY REPORT	Marilyn D. Lopez	Current Date	Page 1 of 2

MH Radiology Report, page 1

MH Radiology Report, page 2

2. THERE WAS A QUESTION OF PREVIOUS SURGERY IN THIS PATIENT, AS THE SUPERIOR ASPECT OF MEDIAL MAXILLARY WALLS WAS NOT WELL DEFINED. WE WERE NOT GIVEN A HISTORY OF PREVIOUS SURGERY.

3. THE LEFT OSTEOMEATAL UNIT WAS NOT WELL VISUALIZED. THE RIGHT WAS DELINEATED; HOWEVER, THIS APPEARED MARKEDLY NARROWED.

1 inch → /Read by/Jerome Lawler, D.L., Radiologist Resident
         /Released by/Daniel Lincoln, M.D., Radiologist

urs/jobxx
c: Shan Chung, M.D.

RADIOLOGY REPORT	Marilyn D. Lopez	Current Date	Page 2 of 2

MH Radiology Report, page 2

HMC Pathology Report

HAYES MEDICAL CENTER
3231 Riverside Drive
Perrysburg, OH 43551-1001

Phone 419-555-7800   Fax 419-555-7890
Excellence in Medical Service for Over 50 Years

LABORATORY DEPARTMENT

PATHOLOGY REPORT

DATE: Current Date

PATIENT NAME: Peter Walen

AGE: 35

SEX: M

PHYSICIAN: Bruce Patterson, M.D.

DATE OF EXAM: Current Date

SPECIMEN: Mid back skin lesion.

LAB NO.: S-02265

GROSS: Received in formalin is a 2.7 x 1.0 cm tan-white skin segment excised to a depth of 0.8 cm. There is an eccentrically located oblong slightly raised lesion measuring 1.1 x 0.8 cm on the skin surface. Specimen is inked, serially sectioned, and entirely submitted excluding the tip as A and B.

MICROSCOPIC DIAGNOSIS: Skin and subcutaneum from mid back—inflamed seborrheic keratosis.

                        Georgia Hart, Director
                        Laboratory

urs/jobxx

PATHOLOGY REPORT	Peter Walen	Current Date	Page 1 of 1

HMC Pathology Report

Stress Echo Report

HAYES MEDICAL CENTER
3231 Riverside Drive
Perrysburg, OH 43551-1001

Phone 419-555-7800   Fax 419-555-7890
Excellence in Medical Service for Over 50 Years

CARDIOVASCULAR MEDICINE UNIT

STRESS ECHO REPORT

DATE: Current Date

PATIENT NAME: Cynthia Gates

REFERRING PHYSICIAN: Anthony Mercer, M.D.

DATE OF TEST: Current Date

PROTOCOL: Rest and postexercise 2-D images were acquired in the LAX, SAX, and apical 4-chamber and 2-chamber views.

INTERPRETATION:

1. Mild to moderate hypokinesis of inferior and posterior segments on SAX and LAX views and of the inferobasilar segment on 2-chamber view.

2. Improved contractility with exercise with minimal residual hypokinesis in inferoposterior segments, suggesting adequate myocardial perfusion.

                        Jason Karns, M.D.

urs/job27
c: Anthony Mercer, M.D.

STRESS ECHO REPORT	Cynthia Gates	Current Date	Page 1 of 1

Stress Echo Report

Physical Exam Report, page 1

HAYES MEDICAL CENTER
3231 Riverside Drive
Perrysburg, OH 43551-1001
Phone 419-555-7800   Fax 419-555-7890
Excellence in Medical Service for Over 50 Years

INTERNAL MEDICINE UNIT

PHYSICAL EXAMINATION REPORT

DATE: Current Date

NAME: Evan Demoulin

DOB: 5/10/60

PHYSICIAN: Daniel Barnett, M.D.

DATE OF EXAM: Current Date

CHIEF COMPLAINT: Rectal bleeding and hematuria.

HISTORY OF PRESENT ILLNESS: Two months ago following micturition, the patient passed 1 tsp of dark red blood per urethra. Before that, he had noted some red staining of his underwear.

There is no associated dysuria, hematuria, or frequency.

Approximately 1 month ago, the patient developed rectal bleeding. This was described as intermittent and associated with pruritus ani. Bright red blood has been passed since that time intermittently, and is not associated with stooling. The patient noted no pain with defecation. He is having up to 5 bowel movements per day and describes tenesmus.

No history of significant weight loss, anorexia, dysphagia, vomiting, or anal injury was noted.

PRESENT MEDICATIONS: None.

ALLERGIES: No known drug allergies. The patient has been treated in the past for exposure to tuberculosis, but not for tuberculosis itself.

| PHYSICAL EXAM REPORT | Evan Demoulin | Current Date | Page 1 of 3 |

Physical Exam Report, page 2

PAST MEDICAL HISTORY:

Surgeries: No prior surgeries are known.

Accidents and Injuries: The patient was in a motor vehicle accident in 1995. He experienced loss of consciousness and some neck strain without vertebral injury.

FAMILY HISTORY: The patient has 3 sisters and 2 brothers, all of whom are reportedly alive and well. There is no known family history of bowel cancer.

SOCIAL HISTORY: The patient is engaged. He is employed fulltime. He smokes approximately 1 pack of cigarettes per day and drinks nearly 2 qts of beer daily. He has no history of use of illicit drugs.

REVIEW OF SYSTEMS:

0.5 inch → **General:** The patient has lost some weight in recent months and admits this is due to a conscious attempt to reduce weight. He has no fever or night sweats.

Skin: He has no rash or moles.

Head: He reports headaches, which were not discussed on this visit.

Eyes: The patient has a cataract in the left eye and reports eye pain.

Nose: No polyps or nasal discharge were noted.

Cardiorespiratory: No cough, sputum, hemoptysis, chest pain, dyspnea, or wheezing was noted. He has no history of rheumatic fever or hypertension.

GI: As described above. The stools are described as dry and hard. The patient has no history of jaundice.

GU: As described above. There is no prior history of renal calculi. No history of penile discharge or prostatitis was noted.

Musculoskeletal: Positive for back pain.

Metabolic: No history of diabetes, thyroid dysfunction, or hyperlipidemia was indicated.

Hematologic: There is no known history of anemia or lymphadenopathy.

| PHYSICAL EXAM REPORT | Evan Demoulin | Current Date | Page 2 of 3 |

Physical Exam Report, page 3

PHYSICAL EXAMINATION:

Vital Signs: Height 5' 7", weight 170 lb, pulse 60 per minute and regular, respirations 16 per minute, blood pressure with large cuff 88/54.

General: The patient is alert, wellbuilt, wellnourished, and in no apparent distress.

Hands: No clubbing is noted.

HEENT: His pupils are equal and reactive to light. Ophthalmoscopy revealed a cataract in the left eye. The right fundus is within normal limits with sharp disk margins. No hemorrhages or exudates were noted. Sclerae nonicteric. Tympanic membranes are pearly grey bilaterally.

Neck: The neck is supple.

Chest: Clear to auscultation with good air entry bilaterally.

Abdomen: The abdomen is soft, non-tender with no masses; there is no organomegaly and no ascites.

Rectal: Negative for mass. Sphincter tone is normal. A stool hemocult was not performed.

Genitalia: No testicular masses or penile or groin lesions are noted.

Extremities: Dorsalis pedis pulses are +2 and equal. There is no ankle edema.

Neurologic: Cranial nerves 2-12 are grossly intact. Tone is within normal limits. Power 5/5 is noted in all 4 extremities. Coordination by finger-to-nose finger test is within normal limits. Deep tendon reflexes are +2 and symmetrical. Sensation is grossly intact.

Daniel Barnett, M.D.

urs/job110

| PHYSICAL EXAM REPORT | Evan Demoulin | Current Date | Page 3 of 3 |

UNIT 1

Admissions Office

FOCUS ON MEDICAL CAREERS

MEDICAL ASSISTANT

Medical assistants can be divided into two categories: administrative and clinical. An administrative medical assistant is responsible for keeping the office running smoothly. Tasks may include, among others, greeting patients; filing and indexing; preparing and collecting bills; using the telephone; preparing correspondence and forms; processing mail; recordkeeping; scheduling appointments, admissions, or medical procedures; transcribing medical dictation; and processing insurance claims.

A clinical medical assistant aids physicians in the medical treatment of patients. Clinical tasks may include sterilizing instruments, taking vital signs, assisting during physical examinations, drawing blood, applying dressings, maintaining treatment rooms, and doing laboratory procedures.

Objectives

- Type documents from various kinds of copy: typed, rough draft, dictated.
- Format and revise one-page and multipage documents used in a medical office: incoming-patient registration form, merge letters, memos, appointment schedule, living will policy, letters, patient information form.
- Compose a short report.
- Proofread documents, supply necessary capitalization and punctuation, and correct errors.

Terms to Know

allergy	oncology
cardiovascular	reconstructive
dermatology	referral
immunology	surgery
internal	surrogate
living will	urology

You have been hired as a medical office assistant in the Center by Mr. Larry Baynes, administrative office manager. Your first responsibility will be to work in the Admissions Office, where you will become familiar with the basic correspondence and forms used throughout the Center.

When you have completed these tasks, you will be assigned to work in each of the medical specialty areas. While you work in Admissions, you will assist Ms. Connie Lawler, Head of Admissions. She will be your supervisor.

Document Processing

JOB 1: Incoming-Patient Registration Form

Remember to type *job01* as the document code 2 lines after the last line of text. Adding the zero before single-digit job numbers will ensure that they are in consecutive order on your disk.

Save this as *job01* on your blank disk.

Format an incoming-patient registration form with 5 columns on plain paper. The form should fill one page. Use the example as a model.

INCOMING-PATIENT REGISTRATION FORM				
Date _____				
Patient's Name	**Arrival Time**	**Appt. Time**	**Doctor**	**Department**

JOB 2: Composed Report

Save this document as *job02*. Remember to add a document code.

Owen Jones called to ask whether the Center has overnight facilities for patients. Compose and type a brief, two-paragraph report in answer to Mr. Jones's question on plain paper. Use *Lodging and Dining Facilities* as the title. Refer to the Procedures Manual for the correct report format and to review the policy regarding lodging.

Is That a Fact?!

Exercise is good for the heart, lungs, arteries, and veins, as well as bones. Like muscles, bones become stronger when they are physically stressed. Exercise can help to prevent a bone condition called osteoporosis, in which bones lose density, weaken, and become porous and fragile.

Save the form letter as *job03f* and the data as *job03d*. Save the merged letters as *job03-1* through *job03-6*.

Use full names in the address, i.e., *Ms. Cindy Louise Davis* and *Mr. Hyung Lee*. Substitute your initials for *urs*. Use the letterhead already formatted for you on your data disk.

Create merged letters using the patients' names and the form letter that follow. Locate the patients' addresses in the Patient Directory. Type the letter on the Center's letterhead, stored on your data disk as **letterhd.** Center and type ADMISSIONS OFFICE in all caps and bold 2 lines below the horizontal rule of the letterhead. Save the new letterhead as **adlethd** to use for other Admissions Office letters.

Ronald Cichy	**Hyung Lee**
Cindy Davis	**April St. John**
Cynthia Gates	**Doris Zollman**

HAYES MEDICAL CENTER
3231 Riverside Drive
Perrysburg, OH 43551-1001

Phone 419-555-7800   Fax 419-555-7890

Excellence in Medical Service for Over 50 Years

ADMISSIONS OFFICE

<<Current Date>>

<<Title>> <<FirstName>> <<MiddleName>> <<LastName>>
<<Address>>
<<City>>, <<State>> <<Postal Code>>

Dear <<Title>> <<LastName>>:

It is almost time for your annual checkup with Dr. Thomas Eadie. Dr. Eadie has indicated that you will be given a stress test, an electrocardiogram, and an echocardiogram, for which you will need to wear loose clothing. Please call me at 419-555-7800, Extension 7821, to schedule an appointment for next month.

If you have questions about the tests, please call Dr. Eadie's office at 419-555-7800, Extension 7827.

Sincerely yours,

Connie Lawler
Head of Admissions

urs
c: Thomas Eadie, M.D.

Save the memo as job04.

Type this memo to the associate administrators on the Center's memo heading stored on your data disk as ***memo.*** Center and type ADMISSIONS OFFICE in all caps and bold, 2 lines below the horizontal rule. Leave a blank line before the guide words *MEMO TO:, FROM:,* etc. Attach a copy of the incoming-patient registration form completed in Job 1 for each administrator.

HAYES MEDICAL CENTER
3231 Riverside Drive
Perrysburg, OH 43551-1001

Phone 419-555-7800   Fax 419-555-7890

Excellence in Medical Service for Over 50 Years

ADMISSIONS OFFICE

MEMO TO: Nathan Avani, Associate Administrator for Business
Neil Roberts, Associate Administrator for Medicine

FROM: Connie Lawler, Head of Admissions

DATE: Current

SUBJECT: Incoming-Patient Registration Form

Attached is a copy of the revised Incoming-Patient Registration Form.
Mr. Baynes and I believe that the form will help us better manage patients'
appointments.

Please let me know if you have any suggestions for or revisions to the
form. May I have your response by next Friday, (supply correct date).

urs
Attachment

Format an appointment schedule similar to the illustration below on plain paper. Center the entire form vertically and horizontally. Extend the table vertically so that you can continue the time through 4:30.

APPOINTMENT SCHEDULE FOR _____ (date)			
Time	**Doctor**	**Time**	**Doctor**
8:30		8:30	
9:00		9:00	
9:30		9:30	
10:00		10:00	
10:30		10:30	
11:00		11:00	
11:30		11:30	

Is That a Fact?!

A Pap smear is a safe, noninvasive medical procedure in which cellular material is obtained from the uterine cervix and placed on a slide. Processing and evaluation of the smear may detect cervical cancer, precancerous lesions, and infections.

Ms. Lucille Moffett, office assistant in Admissions, drafted a policy entitled *Hayes Medical Center Policy for Recording and Honoring Living Wills.* Type the statement, shown here, on Center letterhead using double spacing. Do not include the unit name on the letterhead.

Policy ^for Recording and Honoring Living Wills

Hayes Medical Center ~~all~~ ~~requires~~ staff members to recognize the right of ~~each~~ *every* comp~~i~~*e*tent adult patient to decide whether to receive or refuse medical treatment. Therefore, it enforces the following policy regarding recording and honoring living wills. ^When an adult patient is admitted for in^patient, home health, outpatient surgery, or recovery care, the patient will be provided ^*with* (1) a written statement of Ohio state law on living wills, (2) a copy of the HMC Policy ~~Regarding~~ *for* Recording and Honoring Living Wills, and (3) a copy of the HMC Living Will Acknowledgment. Each adult patient shall sign the ~~Living Will~~ Acknowledgment, which will be filed in the patient's medical records. Like wise, a living will provided to HMC by a patient will be placed in the patient's medical records.

An attempt by the patient to revoke the directive in the patient's living will shall be honored.
HMC will not discriminate against any patients based on the existence or non-existence of a living will.

If an adult patient is ^*un*able to understand or make health care ^*or* treatment decisions, the center will determine whether an active living will exists for the patient. If an active living will does exist, the Center shall make an ~~reasonable~~ effort to consult with the patient's surrogate about the patient's health care ^*and* treatment decisions.

(over)

Any ~~attending~~ physician who is unwilling or unable to follow the directive stated in the patient's living will shall, without delay, transfer the patient—and/or not hinder the transfer of the patient—to another physician who will follow the directive stated in the patient's living will.

Any staff member of the center who is unable or unwilling to comply with this policy shall not impede or stop any other staff member of the center or the hospital form complying with the policy.

JOB 7: Dictated Memo

Use the current date in this memo.

Transcribe the following memo, which was dictated by Ms. Moffett, office assistant in Admissions. You will need to supply the necessary punctuation and capitalization. Use *Draft of Policy About Living Wills* for the subject.

Since this memo is addressed to several individuals (more than three), type *See Distribution Below* after the words *MEMO TO:*. Then, on the second line after the reference initials or the last notation, type *Distribution:* in italics. Leave one blank line; then type a single-column, alphabetical list of the names at the left margin in regular type.

Type a professional designation, where applicable, after each name (for copies and the distribution list), for example, *Steven Novak, M.D.*

this memo goes to all medical directors ... you can find their names in the staff directory ... with a copy to administrators avani ... novak ... and roberts ... enclosed is a copy of our policy about living wills that incorporates recent revisions ... our legal firm has reviewed this policy and finds that it complies with ohio state law on living will directives ... *(Paragraph)* ... based on the legal firms suggestion ... please review the document and make revisions or suggestions that you feel are necessary ... may i receive your feedback on the document by monday ... *(please give the date of two weeks from today)* ... after i make any necessary revisions ... i will resubmit the policy to our legal firm for review ... *(Paragraph)* ... thank you for your assistance ...

Spell out ordinal numbers that can be expressed in two or fewer words, i.e., *thirty-fifth*.

Ms. Lawler has been asked to speak before the Ohio Hospital Administrators' Association in Columbus next summer. Type the following letter for her on the Center's letterhead. Remember to add *ADMISSIONS OFFICE* at the top of the letter. Use the current date.

Mr. Thomas Geissinger, Executive Director
Ohio Hospital Administrators' Association
1515 Capital Avenue
Columbus, OH 43215

Dear Mr. Geissinger:

Thank you for asking me to be a speaker the 35th annual convention of the Ohio Administrators' Hospital Association in Columbus next summer.

It is a pleasure for me to accept your invitation to discuss Hayes Medical Center admission procedures in light of our adding three new medical areas. The 3 new areas—oncology, surgery, and urology—have resulted in our adding admissions staff as well as the paper trail. Enclosed for your information is a brief brochure on our steps for admission procedures.

Our paperwork has increased significantly.

If at all possible, I would like to:

1.   Speak Friday morning so that I might be able to attend the Regional Administrator's session.

2.   Have several microphones set up throughout the auditorium so that the audience may ask questions.

3.   Be supplies with a large screen and an appropriate overhead projector.

(continued on next page)

I will be happy to send a brief synopses [synopsis] of my talk, prior to the ~~meeting~~ convention, if you wish.

Again, thank you for the opportunity to participate as a speaker at the convention.

Sincerely yours,

Connie Lawler
Head of Admissions

urs
Enclosure
c: Neil Roberts, M.D.

JOB 9: Patient Information Form

Ms. Moffett has drafted a new patient information form for you to format. Leave a 1-inch top margin and use Times New Roman 10 pt for everything but the heading.

HAYES MEDICAL CENTER — (bold) — PATIENT ~~DATA~~ INFORMATION
3231 Riverside Drive
Perrysburg, OH 43551-1001
419-555-7800

PLEASE PRINT YOUR ANSWERS. RETURN THIS FORM TO THE (bold)
RECEPTIONIST.

PATIENT'S NAME _____ Use a small font _____
       Last   First   Initial

STREET ADDRESS _____

CITY _____ STATE _____ ZIP _____

HOME PHONE NO. [NO.#] _____ WORK ~~TELEPHONE~~ PHONE NO. _____

BIRTHDATE [#] _____ AGE _____ SEX ___ SS NO. _____ Increase length

MARITAL STATUS: SINGLE ___ MARRIED ___ WIDOW [WIDOWED] ___ DIVORCED ___

(continued on next page)

FAMILY DOCTOR AND ADDRESS _____

_____

REFERRAL SOURCE AND ADDRESS _____

Insert a heavy line → YOUR EMPLOYER _____

EMPLOYER'S ADDRESS _____

IF YOU ARE A MINOR, PLEASE PROVIDE THE FOLLOWING INFORMATION:

FATHER'S NAME _____

ADDRESS _____

FATHER'S EMPLOYER _____

Employer's ADDRESS _____

MOTHER'S NAME _____

MOTHER'S ADDRESS _____

MOTHER'S EMPLOYER _____

Employer's ADDRESS _____

add a heavy line ARE YOU BEING SEEN FOR A WORK RELATED INJURY? YES___ NO___

ARE YOU BEING SEEN AS THE RESULT OF AN AUTO RELATED INJURY?
YES_____ NO_____

Begin a new page. Center and type (over) at the bottom of page 1.

(continued on next page)

INSURANCE INFORMATION

<u>Primary Insurance</u> NAME _____

Policy NO.   *Group No.*   POLICY HOLDER'S NAME _____

INSURANCE COMPANY'S ADDRESS _____

SECONDARY INSURANCE NAME _____

POLICY NO. _____ *Group No.* POLICY HOLDER'S NAME _____

INSURANCE COMPANYS ADDRESS _____

_____

add a heavy line   WE SUBMIT INSURANCE CLAIMS FOR OUR PATIENTS.

HOW ~~DO~~ *WILL* YOU ~~PLAN ON~~ PAYING FOR YOUR OFFICE VISIT TODAY?

CASH _____ CHECK _____ VISA(R)_____ ☐ MASTERCARD(R) _____

I HEREBY AUTHORI*Z*SE REL*A*EASE OF INFORMATION NECESSARY TO

FILE A CLAIM WITH MY INSURANCE C*C*OMPANY AND ASSIGN *TO*

BENEFITS OTHERWISE PAYABLE TO ME TO THE ~~DOCTOR~~ *PHYSICIAN* OR TO THE

CENTER AS INDICATED ON THE CLAIM. A COPY OF THE SIGNATURE

IS AS VALID AS THE OR*I*G*I*NAL.

SIGNATURE OF PAT*IE*NT OR RESPONS*I*ABLE PARTY

_____

DATE _____

Is That a Fact?!

The immune system of the human body helps keep the body healthy by fighting germs and diseases. HIV, Human Immunodeficiency Virus, is a virus that attacks the immune system. HIV can disable the body's immune system and evolve into AIDS, Acquired Immune Deficiency Syndrome.

JOB 10: Dictated Memo

Remember to type an attachment notation.

Use a distribution list similar to the one in Job 7.

Indicate separate possession by adding an apostrophe to the name of each person, i.e., *Connie Lawler's and Nathan Avani's assistance.*

Transcribe the following memo that Ms. Moffett dictated.

this memo goes to all administrators . . . and all the heads of medical and other units . . . please supply the necessary punctuation and capitalization . . . use the subject . . . new patient information form . . . attached is a draft of the new patient information form i have developed with connie lawlers and nathan avanis assistance . . . we think this form is a sound improvement over our current admission form . . . *(Paragraph)* . . . please mark any suggestions or other information that you feel might be useful on the form . . . may i have your revisions by monday *(date of one week from today)* . . . thank you . . .

Portfolio

Revise the Policy for Recording and Honoring Living Wills if you have errors in it. Then resave it as *port1*. Print one copy for your portfolio.

UNIT 2 Head and Neck

Objectives

- Type documents from various kinds of copy: typed, handwritten, dictated.
- Create letterhead and memo heading for unit.
- Format and revise one-page and multipage documents used in a head and neck office: summary of ENG findings, memo, note to patient file, merge letters, authorization for release of medical information, consultation report, pathology report, medical note, radiology report.
- Compose a short report.
- Proofread documents; supply necessary capitalization and punctuation; and correct errors.

Terms to Know

acanthosis	endotracheal	myringotomy	otolaryngological
adenoidectomy	epistaxis	nares	palpated
aeruginosa	ethmoid	nasopharyngolaryngoscope	paranasal
aphonia	hyperkeratosis	nasopharynx	supraglottis
cryptic	hypertrophic	nystagmus	turbinates
dysplasia	lymphocytes	ossicles	tympanomeatal
edematous	mastoid	osteomeatal	tympanplasty
electronystagmogram	mucosa	otitis media	

ORIENTATION

Today you will begin working in the Head and Neck Unit. You will be assisting Dr. Thomas Ziss, director; Dr. Chris O'Dell; Ms. Leslie A. Scott, Audiologist; and Ms. Diane Oaster, office assistant. Ms. Oaster will be your supervisor.

The physicians and specialists in the unit specialize in otolaryngology—the diagnosis and treatment of ear, nose, and throat disorders. Surgery on the head, neck, and face is performed at Memorial Hospital. The Laboratory and Radiology Departments as well as the Head and Neck Unit are sites used for testing. Some outpatient surgeries are performed within the outpatient surgery unit.

The reports for the Center and for Memorial Hospital both follow a particular format. Variations from this format, if any, will be provided with the job instructions.

Ms. Oaster has asked that you review the Procedures Manual for several items: formats, multipage documents, page numbering, closing lines of medical reports, number usage, and capitalization of generic and chemical names of medications and drugs.

In order to avoid possible misreading of technical data, Ms. Oaster explained that all significant numbers and statistics should be typed in figures and symbols, not in words.

Supply the necessary capitalization and punctuation for all correspondence that has been dictated. You may find it helpful first to read the dictation. As always, proofread your work carefully.

NOTE: The patient data file is introduced in this unit. A patient data file begins with a summary of the preliminary examination of a patient. As time passes, additional data relating to the patient's surgery and follow-up are added to the file. These records enable the physician to see the patient's full medical history as provided by that physician or the medical unit over a period of time.

You will be asked to supply specified dates or the current date for these notes. You will gain a sense of sequence as you follow the treatment of patients from preliminary visits through surgery and final follow-up reexamination. Use a current calendar to supply the dates in all documents.

Document Processing

JOB 11: Head and Neck Unit Letterhead

Create a letterhead named *headlet* for the Head and Neck Unit. Retrieve the Hayes Medical Center letterhead from your data disk. Two lines below the horizontal rule, center and type *HEAD AND NECK UNIT* in all caps and bold. The Center letterhead will be used for all of the units and will be identical except for the different unit names. Use this letterhead with the correct unit name for all unit letters and reports.

JOB 12: Summary of ENG Findings

Refer to the Procedures Manual for the correct report format.

Dr. Barnett referred Julia Mae Falk to the Head and Neck Unit for diagnosis of her repeated dizzy spells. Ms. Scott, the audiologist, performed an ENG test today to see if a hearing disorder might be the cause of the dizziness. Prepare the following report. Use ENG summary in the footer.

Remember to type the document code on the last page.

Summary of ENG Findings

Date:

Patient: Julia Mae Falk

Saccade Test: Essentially negative except for poor latencies bilaterally (patient's age may be a factor).

Gaze Test: Negative.

Pendular Tracking: Within normal limits.

Optokinetic Tracking: Symmetrical.

Dix Hallpike Test: There was low-intensity, right beating throughout both maneuvers. No dizziness was noted on Hallpike left; latent dizziness on Hallpike right.

Positional Nystagmus: Low-intensity, right beating in several positions.

Bithermal Calorics: Differential excitability within normal limits.

Spontaneous Nystagmus: Low-intensity, right beating (8° per second).

Nystagmus Fixation: Normal suppression.

Impression: The electronystagmogram (ENG) reveals a low-intensity, right beating, spontaneous nystagmus, which is also noted on Positional Testing and Dix Hallpike testing. These abnormal findings are of nonlocalizing pathology.

No evidence on the ENG suggests a peripheral vestibular disorder. The patient's audiogram demonstrates a moderate sensorineural hearing loss of the right ear. The audiogram demonstrates a moderate to severe sensorineural hearing loss of the left ear with fair discrimination.

If the symptoms remain, neurologic and/or metabolic testing might be considered.

c: Daniel Barnett, M.D.

JOB 13: Head and Neck Unit Memo Heading

Is That a Fact?!

The four types of hearing loss are conductive, sensory, neural, and central. Each type is named for the area of the ear that is affected.

Ms. Oaster would like you to create the Head and Neck memo heading, to be named *headmemo*. It should be typed on Hayes Medical Center letterhead with the words *HEAD AND NECK UNIT* centered and typed in all caps and bold 2 lines below the horizontal rule. Be sure to leave a blank line between the unit name and the words *MEMO TO:*.

Read the entire memo before beginning to type. Supply the appropriate dates.

Type the following memo, which informs all directors of the annual blood drive. Include your name with Ms. Oaster's in the heading.

Memo To: All Directors

From: Diane Oaster and (Your Name)

Date: (Current)

Subject: Annual Red Cross Blood Drive

In cooperation with our regional Red Cross office, we will hold our Annual Red Cross Blood Drive on (complete date one month from today). The drive will begin at 9:30 a.m. and continue until 3 p.m. in Laboratory Rooms 23 and 25 of the Surgery Unit.

We all know the importance of having an adequate supply of blood for medical uses and emergency situations. As always, we encourage our employees and staff to participate in this important health program.

If you are able to assist with the drive either in the morning or afternoon of (correct date), please call one of us. We anticipate a large number of donors.

Please join us in the worthy cause of donating blood.

Is That a Fact?!

Immunizations, or vaccinations, help create immunity to certain infections. They are developed with relatively harmless antigens, or molecules. These antigens originate from or are similar to microorganisms that cause diseases.

JOB 15: Operative Report

For paragraphs of four or more lines, leave at least two lines on the previous page and carry at least two lines to the new page.

Ms. Oaster has asked you to assist her in typing the following report on Arthur Gossman. Type the report on the Center's form that is stored on your data disk as **medrec**. Refer to the Procedures Manual for the correct format. The operation was performed today in one of the unit examining rooms. Copies should be noted for each of Mr. Gossman's three physicians.

Operative Report

Date:

Patient Name: Arthur Gossman

Surgeon: Chris O'Dell, M.D.

Operation: Diagnostic nasal endoscopy.

Preop Diagnosis: Left ethmoid maxillary sinusitis.

Postop Diagnosis: Same.

Procedure: The patient was placed in the examining chair in a sitting position. Each of the nares was sprayed with $\frac{1}{2}$% NeoSynephrine, which was followed by 4% topical Xylocaine. Cotton pledgets soaked in a similar solution were placed up into the middle meatus in each naris bilaterally. After a sufficient amount of waiting time, each of the pledgets was removed. Each of the nares was then inspected with the 30° and the 70° scopes. I found the patient's septum to be midline, and inspection of the right naris revealed normal anatomy with normal turbinates. The middle meatus also was normal. Passage of the scope into the middle meatus revealed no polyps, crusting, pus, or excessive secretions. The scopes were then used in the left naris. The patient showed evidence of having a previous ethmoidectomy. In addition, the anterior aspect of the middle turbinate was missing. The middle meatus revealed no polyps, crusting, thick drainage, or other secretions.

I was easily able to inspect the natural os area, and inspection into this area revealed a normal maxillary sinus. I noted that the remaining portion of the middle turbinate was retracted against the lateral wall of the left naris, and in the anterior superior aspect above the natural os area in the ethmoid, there was some thick mucoid drainage. This was clear and was removed with suction. No other abnormalities were noted in this area.

The scope was then directed into the inferior meatus. I noted a large, open antrostomy site in this area as well. The mucosa was noted to be normal, without polyps, crusting, or cysts.

The patient tolerated the procedure well and left the office in a satisfactory condition.

c: Sebastian Avery, M.D.

Abraham Jones, M.D.

Annie Pitman, M.D.

JOB 16: Merged Letters

When addressing a girl younger than 13 years of age, omit the personal title *Miss* or *Ms.* In this case, use the first name and the surname in the salutation, i.e., *Dear Ashleigh Damon:*.

Create a form file, and name it *job16f,* to contain the form letter that follows. Then, create a data file, and name it *job16d,* to contain the patient information for the patients listed below. Save the merged letters as *job16a* through *job16c.* (You will prepare the enclosure in Job 17.)

> Ashleigh Damon (List *Mrs. Louise Damon, Guardian,* on the second line of the inside address.)
> Sherry Davis
> Pamela Haggerty

You can find their addresses in the patient directory.

<<Current Date>>

<<Title>> <<First Name>> <<Middle Name>> <<Last Name>>
<<Parent/Guardian>>
<<Address1>>
<<City>>, <<State>> <<PostalCode>>

Dear <<Title>> <<First Name>> <<LastName>>:
You have been scheduled for surgery by the Head and Neck Unit of Hayes Medical Center next month. Enclosed is a copy of a form that permits your physician to release your medical history to us. Hayes Medical Center requires this vital health information to eliminate repeat preoperative tests and, thus, reduce time and costs involved.

Please provide the name of your physician or medical group and your date of birth on the form. After you sign and date the form, deliver it to your physician so that your medical history will be forwarded to us prior to your surgery.

If you need additional forms for other physicians, please call the Center at 419-555-7800.

Sincerely yours,

Thomas Ziss, M.D., Director
Head and Neck Unit

urs
Enclosure

A physician must refer to the full medical history of patients in order to prescribe an accurate health program for them. This written history often must be obtained from other physicians.

Format the Authorization for Release of Medical Information illustrated. Use Center letterhead. Create the rules using the table feature so that you can fill in the correct information in later jobs.

AUTHORIZATION FOR RELEASE OF MEDICAL INFORMATION

In an effort to avoid duplication, and thereby help control costs, I hereby authorize and request

_____

Physician or Medical Group

to release the following information contained in my records, including information about Human Immune Deficiency Virus Positivity (HIV+), Acquired Immune Deficiency Syndrome (AIDS), and AIDS-Related Complex (ARC), as defined by the Ohio Department of Public Health.

_____

Patient Name   **Date of Birth**

_____ History and Physical   _____ X-ray/MRI Report
_____ Laboratory Reports   _____ Surgery Report
_____ Pathology Reports   _____ Progress Report
_____ Audiology Reports   _____ All Medical Records
_____ Discharge Summary   _____ Treatment Summary
_____ Other

To:_____
_____
_____
_____

I understand that I may revoke this authorization at any time and that it automatically expires once the purpose for which it was intended is accomplished. My signature means that I have read this form and/or have had it read to me and explained in language that I can understand.

_____

Signature of Patient, Parent, or Guardian   **Today's Date**

JOB 18: Authorizations for Release of Medical Information

Do not replace the form you created in Job 17 with the filled-in forms.

Type individual copies of the Authorization for Release of Medical Information for the patients listed in Job 16. Save the copies as *job18a*, *job18b*, and *job18c*, respectively. On each form add the patient name, check *All Medical Records*, and provide Dr. Ziss's name and address.

JOB 19: Dictated Consultation Letter

Remember to refer to the Procedures Manual for correct formats.

A consultation letter is used by a medical specialist to provide information to a physician in planning the medical management of a patient's health.

Ms. Oaster explained that the subject line and patient's date of birth (e.g., *RE: Sherry Davis* and *DOB: 5/5/54*) are typed 2 lines below the salutation in bold on separate lines.

Dr. Lyons referred Sherry Davis to the Head and Neck Unit for further examination and treatment of recurring tonsillitis. Dr. Ziss dictated this consultation report of the examination and subsequent removal of the patient's tonsils and adenoids. Transcribe the report.

Transcribe *miz* as *Ms.*, a term used to address a woman of whom the marital status is unknown or at a woman's request.

> **Send this letter to doctor jerome k lyons . . . 867 hubbell street . . . maumee ohio . . . 43537 . . . 1002 . . . dear doctor lyons . . . regarding sherry davis . . . date of birth . . . 5 . . . 5 . . . 54 . . . i examined sherry davis . . . a 45 year old female who presented to us with a history of tonsillitis . . . examination revealed cryptic . . . chronically infected tonsils and adenoids . . . examination of the oral cavity . . . hypopharynx . . . and larynx were otherwise within normal limits . . . because this has been medically refractory to treatment . . . we proceeded with a tonsillectomy and adenoidectomy . . . (*Paragraph*) . . . postoperatively the patient is doing very well . . . we hope this will afford miz davis some lasting improvement . . . (*Paragraph*) . . . thank you very much for this referral . . .**

Is That a Fact?!

Migraine is a neurological disorder characterized by recurring headaches. Pain usually occurs on one side of the head, along with one or more other symptoms. These symptoms may include nausea, vomiting, and sensitivity to light and sound. Migraine medication may give relief by "quieting" sensitive nerve pathways and reducing the inflammation of blood vessels around the brain.

Use figures and symbols, rather than words, when typing medical facts and statistics, e.g., 0.7 × 0.5 × 0.2 cm.

The Laboratory Department has asked you to assist in formatting this pathology report on a specimen of Robert Hatfield's left ear. Two lines below the Center's letterhead, center and type *LABORATORY DEPARTMENT* in all caps and bold. Space down two times and center and type the name of the report in all caps, bold, and underlined. See the Procedures Manual for the Center's format.

Date:

Name: Robert Hatfield

Age: 66

Sex: M

Physician: Thomas Ziss, M.D.

Date of Exam: (*Use today's date.*)

Specimen: Biopsy, left ear.

Lab. No.: S-7195-85

Gross: Specimen is composed of three portions of brown-red, soft tissue measuring 0.7 x 0.5 x 0.2 cm. The entire specimen is sectioned and is submitted in total.

Microscopic: The sections reveal a stratified squamous epithelium with acanthosis and hyperkeratosis. The underlying supporting tissues are severely edematous and hyperemic. This edematous tissue is infiltrated by chronic inflammatory cells consisting mostly of mature plasma cells, but occasional histiocytes and small, round lymphocytes are noted. There is no evidence of malignancy.

Diagnosis: Biopsy, left ear—chronically inflamed granulation tissue.

Georgia Hart
Pathologist

Some medical forms require portions to be typed in all caps, as shown.

Dr. O'Dell referred James Church to the Radiology Department for a CT scan. The Radiology Department uses the facilities at Memorial Hospital for CT scans.

Prepare the report shown using the Memorial Hospital Department of Radiology form stored on your data disk as *membrad*.

Type the closing lines (*/ Read By /* and so on) 4 lines below the body and 1 inch from the left margin. Type your reference initials and the document code 2 lines below the last line.

Patient: James Church
Medical Record No. S000202032
DOB: 2/6/50
Room: OP
Physician: Keith Anderson, M.D.
Ordering Physician: Chris O'Dell, M.D.
Billing Code, 99994; Billing No., S13554837; Exam No., 2351
DESCRIPTION: CT SCAN OF BRAIN
INDICATION: SINUSITUS.
CT SCAN OF BRAIN: CT imaging of the paranasal sinuses was performed in the direct coronal projection without contrast enhancement. The examination shows marked mucosal membrane thickening of the ethmoids bilaterally but perhaps greater on the right. There is also extensive mucosal membrane thickening in both maxillary sinuses, again probably a little bit greater on the right. The frontal sinuses are rather small and poorly pneumatized. There is mucosal membrane thickening of the right sphenoid sinus. This is a minimal amount of thickening.

No air fluid levels are seen. The osteomeatal units appear to be obstructed bilaterally.

The bony nasal septum deviates slightly to the left in its lower course. There is some enlargement or thickening of the inferior and medial turbinate on the right side as compared to the left. The possibility of polyps in the nose cannot be excluded.

IMPRESSION:
BILATERAL ETHMOID AND MAXILLARY SINUSITIS WITH THE CHANGES BEING MOST PRONOUNCED ON THE RIGHT. THE OSTEOMEATAL UNITS APPEAR OBSTRUCTED.

/Read By/ Keith Anderson, M.D., Radiologist
/Released By/ Keith Anderson, M.D., Radiologist

Ms. Scott has asked you to type this patient data file concerning Glenna Lambert's voice problem. Refer to the Procedures Manual for the correct format. Mrs. Lambert's date of birth is 6/28/58. Use Ms. Scott's name and title as the physician. Mrs. Lambert's chief complaint is loss of voice. Use the current date.

The patient is a 42-year-old female. She was seen by Dr. Alyssa R. DeWeese, her family physician, and under her recommendation, has undergone approximately 2 months of voice rest. Medical records indicate that she scheduled her appointment with Dr. Ziss in order to get a "second opinion." She is now a patient of Dr. Ziss. Results of his nasopharyngolaryngoscopy done under topical anesthesia revealed a "slight nodule on the anterior aspect of the right vocal cord." There is no evidence of any vocal cord lesion; her vocal fold motility was considered to be "good."

Subjective evaluation of her voice today reveals an array of symptoms associated with vocal nodules. Her dysphonia is characterized by severe hoarseness that is complicated by periods of diplophonia, low pitch, and pitch breaks. Respiratory control for speech needs is inefficient. Voice onset does not coincide with peak of inhalation, and she continues to talk when adequate breath support is not available. Speech rate is rapid for conversational contacts, and during lengthy utterances she changes the position of her neck to protrude the mandible in an effort to perpetuate voicing. Voicing near the end of an utterance is typified by pitch breaks and an audible tremor. Calculation of an s/z ratio is consistent with benign vocal fold lesions. Ratios for 2 trials consisted of 2.0 and 1.7, respectively.

(continued on next page)

Is That a Fact?!

The thyroid gland monitors growth rate and metabolism. During and after pregnancy, the body's hormones and immune system can change. Sometimes this results in development of a thyroid condition. Only about 1 in 500 pregnant women actually develop a thyroid condition, which often resolves itself.

A period of trial therapy emphasizing breath control and sequencing of inhalation and voice onset produced audible changes in voicing. Mrs. Lambert was able to recognize changes in her vocal quality, and for brief periods she was able to sustain clear voicing for approximately 3 seconds. She was provided with information on a vocal hygiene program. Continuing voice therapy was recommended with emphasis to be directed at breath control and support for speech needs, recognition of body postures suitable for improved speech, awareness of vocal hygiene, cueing strategies regarding ways to manage periods when her voicing deteriorates, and emphasis on the use of phrases and pauses during spontaneous speech.

A voice recording was made this afternoon. She should return again in 2 weeks for a follow-up visit.

Portfolio

Revise the consultation report if you have any errors in it. Resave it as *port2*. Print one copy for your portfolio.

Cardiovascular Medicine

FOCUS ON MEDICAL CAREERS

EKG TECHNICIAN

An EKG technician is trained to use an electrocardiograph, which detects and records electronic impulses transmitted by the heart muscle. The technician may assist in monitoring the heart during diagnostic and therapeutic procedures and heart catheterization.

Because the work of an EKG technician is associated with the cardiovascular system, the technician must be knowledgeable about the anatomy and physiology of the system and the abnormalities and treatments for diseases of the system.

Objectives

- Type documents from various kinds of copy: typed, rough draft, dictated.
- Create letterhead for unit.
- Format and revise one-page and multipage documents used in a cardiovascular office: exercise test patient consent form, discharge summary, test reports (exercise treadmill with echo, stress echo, echocardiogram), information sheet, hospital medical record form letters, return visit report, history and physical report, operative report letters.
- Proofread documents; supply necessary capitalization, punctuation, salutations, and closing lines; and correct errors.

Terms to Know

anastomosis	cholesterol	exertional	pectoris
angioplasty	claudication	femoral	percutaneous
arrhythmia	congestion	fibrillation	prandial
atherectomy	contractility	fluoroscope	Procardia
auscultation	diaphoresis	hyperlipidemia	reoccluded
bradycardia	dyspnea	hypokinesis	reperfusion
Capoten	echocardiography	ischemia	restenosis
cardiolite	endarterectomy	myocardial	systolic
cardiopulmonary	epithelium	nitroglycerin	thallium
catheterization	erythromycin	normocephalic	

ORIENTATION

Today you will begin working in the Cardiovascular Medicine Unit. You will work with Dr. Jeffrey Szabo, director; Dr. Thomas Eadie; Dr. Jason Karns; and Mr. Curt Thomas, office assistant. Mr. Thomas will be your supervisor.

The physicians and specialists in the unit specialize in the diagnosis and treatment of heart disorders. They do consultative cardiology, noninvasive cardiovascular procedures, cardiac catheterization, and coronary angioplasty. Testing is performed in the Laboratory and Radiology Departments. Surgery is conducted at Memorial Hospital as well as in the Center's outpatient clinic. Various stress tests are conducted in the unit examining rooms.

Documents that are unique to the Cardiovascular Unit will include formatting directions. Otherwise, refer to the Procedures Manual for formats.

Mr. Thomas has indicated that detailed instructions for documents that you have formatted before will not be repeated unless necessary. Be sure to capitalize the names of medications and become familiar with specialized terms and names of tests, equipment, and so on.

Document Processing

JOB 23: Cardiovascular Medicine Unit Letterhead

Create a letterhead and name it *cardlet* for the Cardiovascular Medicine Unit. The letterhead should be identical to the Center letterhead except that *CARDIOVASCULAR MEDICINE UNIT* is centered and typed in all caps and bold 2 lines below the horizontal line.

Use the letterhead for all Unit letters and to begin all Hayes Medical Center reports and other documents for the Unit.

Is That a Fact?!

Heart failure is a condition in which the heart becomes enlarged and stops pumping blood efficiently. Some of its symptoms include shortness of breath, fainting, and fluid accumulation. It is thought that the disease may run in families. Early recognition and medical treatment may help slow its progression.

JOB 24: Exercise Test Consent Form

Remember to type an identifying document code.

A patient consent form grants permission to the unit physicians to conduct exercise tests on patients. A patient's signature on this form indicates that he or she understands the test and the possibility of certain physical or medical changes.

Type the form on unit letterhead. Type the title of the form 2 lines below the unit name in all caps, bold, and underlined.

Exercise Test
Patient Consent Form

NAME: _____
               Last   **First**   **Initial**

In order to determine an appropriate plan of medical management, I hereby consent to voluntarily engage in an exercise test to determine the state of my heart and circulation. Before I undergo the test, I will have an interview with a physician. I also will be examined by a physician to determine if I have a condition that would indicate I should not engage in the test.

The test that I will undergo will be performed on a treadmill or bicycle, with the amount of effort increasing gradually. The increase in effort will continue until symptoms such as fatigue, shortness of breath, or chest discomfort appear, indicating that exercise should stop.

During the performance of the test, a physician and technologist will monitor my pulse, blood pressure, and electrocardiogram tracing.

The possibility exists of certain changes occurring during the test. These include abnormal blood pressure, fainting, disorders of heartbeat (too rapid, too slow, or ineffective), and very rare instance of heart attack. Every effort will be made to minimize these risks by preliminary examination and by observations during the test. Emergency equipment and trained personnel will be available to deal with unusual situations that may arise.

The information obtained during the test will be treated as privileged and confidential and will be released only to my physician unless my written consent is given.

I have read the foregoing and I understand it. Any questions that have occurred to me have been answered to my satisfaction.

SIGNED _____ **DATE** _____
WITNESS _____

Save this summary as *job25* before you begin typing.

Type the physicians' full names followed by *M.D.* in the heading and closing lines.

Type the dates in the headings in number format, i.e., *00/00/00*.

Type the report title in all caps, bold, and underlined.

Familiarize yourself with the medical abbreviations, terms, and phrases. You will use them frequently as you progress through the Center.

Type each medication on a separate line.

Medications to which a patient is allergic are typed in all caps and bold so that they can be noted quickly and clearly.

Louise Cox was taken to Memorial Hospital's Emergency Room yesterday because she was experiencing severe chest pains. Dr. Eadie, her cardiologist, was called. Dr. James Baker, Emergency Room, Memorial Hospital, discharged Ms. Cox the same day and then filed the following summary.

Type the summary on the Memorial Hospital Medical Record Form (*medrec*). Be sure to supply the patient's name, physician, room number, history number, and type of report. Verify that the pages are numbered correctly.

Physician: Thomas Eadie, M.D.

Room No.: DIS

History No: 255081

Admitted:

Discharged:

Dictated:

Admission Diagnosis: Chest pain.

Hospital Course: This patient is a 44-year-old female with a 5-day history of chest pain described as slow in onset, substernal in location, with radiation to her right arm and right shoulder intermittently and with some right jaw pain. She had taken a total of 8 sublingual nitroglycerin, which gave only mild relief. This pain was not associated with any diaphoresis, shortness of breath, or syncope; she had no vomiting. She had developed some degree of nausea during this occurrence. She had called Dr. Szabo's office on the day of admission about her pain. Dr. Szabo told the patient to come to the Emergency Room for further workup and evaluation.

Past Medical History: She had coronary artery bypass graft × 3 in 1994, × 2 in 1995, and × 2 in 1996 with a history of 3 mild heart infarctions and 3 angioplasties. She also has a history of a peptic ulcer. After reclosure of STAT PTCA, her vein graft was circumflexed for acute MI in December of 1996. Her left internal mammary artery, failed to her left anterior descending through a 60–70% vein graft to her LAD, remained patent last week. A stenosis of 90% was noted at anastomosis of her new third graft; it was dilated 9 days prior. Her cardiac risks are as above. She has high cholesterol.

Allergies: She is allergic to IODINE, DEMEROL, DARVON, NORGESIC, CLEOCIN, ERYTHROMYCIN.

Medications: Pepcid 40 mg 1 tablet p.o. ad. Mevacor 40 mg 1 tablet p.o. b.i.d. Cardene 20 mg 1 tablet p.o. t.i.d. Vasotec 2.5 mg q.i.d. Premarin 0.625 mg 1 tablet p.o. q.i.d. 1 baby aspirin q.i.d.

Family History: Negative. No diabetes, hypertension.

Social History: She is a smoker.

(continued on next page)

Review of Systems: Negative for any fever, chills, night sweats. No history of any pulmonary, gastrointestinal, genitourinary, or any CNS abnormalities.

Physical Exam:

> **Vital Signs:** Temperature is 98.6. Pulse 79 and regular with no ectopy on the monitor in the Emergency Department. Respirations were 18 and unlabored.

> **Blood pressure** was 92/53.

> **General:** This is a well-developed, mildly obese female, alert and oriented to person, place, and time, and in no apparent distress. Denies any chest pain during history-taking.

> **HEENT:** PERRLA. EOMI. Fundi show a sharp cup/disk ratio. No sinus tenderness. Oral exam shows no acute infection.

> **Neck:** Supple. No palpable masses. No audible bruits.

> **Chest:** Clear to auscultation bilaterally with mild crackles in her right lower lobe on inspiration. No A to E changes.

> **Cor:** Regular rate and rhythm. Heart sounds are distant. No audible murmur. No rubs.

> **Extremities:** The patient has +1/4 edema to her right lower leg, and she is status post trauma to that leg. There is no edema on her left leg.

Laboratory: During time of Emergency Room assessment, her EKG shows a sinus rhythm with Q waves in 2 AVF and a mild amount of ST elevation in V2 and V3, which shows change from her previous EKGs several months prior to this admission day. No blood labs were back at this time. Chest x-ray was pending.

Assessment and Plan: Chest pain in lieu of patient's multiple cardiac history. She is to be admitted to CCU within the next week to rule out myocardial infarction and to obtain CPK and enzymes. In discussion with Dr. Eadie, the patient was started on heparin therapy and will check TCTs and PTT level to rule out possible stenosis or occlusion to her coronary artery.

James F. Baker, M.D.

c: Thomas Eadie, M.D.

Type the date in
figure style.

Dr. Anthony Mercer referred Cynthia Gates to Dr. Karns. Ms. Gates was experiencing chest pains, and she has coronary disease. Under Dr. Karns's direction today, Ms. Gates's heart was monitored while she was on a treadmill.

Type the physician's report on unit letterhead. In the footer, use *ECHO REPORT* as the document name.

Exercise Treadmill with Echo Report

Name: Cynthia Gates

Date of Test:

Referring Physician: Anthony Mercer, M.D.

Indication for Testing: The patient is a 50-year-old female who is undergoing evaluation for chest pain and coronary disease.

Examination: Resting pulse was 78 beats per minute. Blood pressure was 126/80 mm/Hg. The lungs were clear. There was a soft systolic ejection murmur along the left sternal border.

EKG: The patient's resting, modified, 12-lead EKG had no resting abnormalities.

Protocol: The patient was exercised with a Bruce protocol in conjunction with stress echocardiography. She exhibited excellent exercise tolerance, exercising a total of 9 minutes and 30 seconds, which equates to an estimated 11 MET. The patient achieved 86% of her predicted maximum heart rate. The test was terminated at achievement of target heart rate. At the peak of exercise there was < 1 mm of ST depression in leads II, III, AVF. On the 1-minute postexercise tracing there was no ST depression. The patient had no exercise-associated arrhythmias.

Final Comments:

1. Negative exercise treadmill for ischemia to 11 MET, and > 85% predicted maximum heart rate.
2. Please also see stress echo report.

Jason Karns, M.D.

c: Anthony Mercer, M.D.

Type the report on unit letterhead.

Dr. Karns administered a stress echo test to Cynthia Gates. Type the results of that test, which was conducted today. Send a copy to Dr. Mercer.

Stress Echo Report

Date:

Name: Cynthia Gates

Date of Test:

Referring Physician: Anthony Mercer, M.D.

Protocol: Rest and postexercise 2-D images were acquired in the LAX, SAX, and apical 4-chamber and 2-chamber views.

Interpretation:

1. **Mild to moderate hypokinesis of inferior and posterior segments on SAX and LAX views and of the inferobasilar segment on 2-chamber view.**
2. **Improved contractility with exercise with minimal residual hypokinesis in inferoposterior segments, suggesting adequate myocardial perfusion.**

                                      Jason Karns, M.D.

c: Anthony Mercer, M.D.

Is That a Fact?!

For transmission of HIV to occur, HIV must pass from the body fluids or tissue of one person to those of another person. Health care workers who may come into contact with a patient's blood or body fluids should follow precautions to prevent HIV transmission.

Mr. Thomas asked you to type a final copy of the following information sheet on preparing a dobutamine thallium test. Type the form on unit letterhead with single spacing.

DOBUTAMINE TEST WITH THALLIUM

PATIENT NAME _____

APPOINTMENT DATE _____   TIME_____

Please follow these instructions:

1. You may park in the visitor's parking lot located on Riverside Drive in front of the Center, where ~~where~~ *Free* valet parking is available.

2. Report to the Admitting Department of the Center's Outpatient Clinic ~~thirty~~ *30* minutes prior to your scheduled appointment. ~~Once~~ *After* your paperwork is completed, you will be directed to the Cardiovascular Unit located on the second floor.

Please remember:

• Do not eat 4 hours prior to your scheduled appointment. *You may* ~~D~~isregard this if you are a diabetic. *— or drink anything except water*

• Continue use of all medications.

• Wear loose fitting clothing and walking shoes or sneakers.

• The first portion of this test will take about 1 hour.

• Approximately 4 hours later, you will return to the Cardiovascular waiting area for the second set of images, which will take about 30 minutes.

• *all caps —* During the 4-hour waiting period between tests, do not eat. However, you may drink liquids, such as water or decaffeinated coffee or beverages. You may disregard this instruction if you are a diabetic.

• If you are unable to keep your scheduled appointment or if you have any questions regarding this test, please call our office at 555-7825.

JOB 29: Dictated Consultation Letter

Type the date in a combination of words and numbers.

Type the physician's full name followed by *M.D.* in the inside address. Use *Dr.* and the last name in the salutation.

Use *RE:* for the subject line in all patient-related letters.

Do not use commas to set off expressions that are essential to the completeness of a sentence (that identify a particular subject or item), e.g., *your patient Angela Lopez.*

Insert commas after introductory phrases that precede the subject and verb.

Dr. Raymond Lewis referred his patient, Angela Lopez, to Dr. Karns for consultation. Dr. Karns found it necessary to perform a coronary angioplasty on Ms. Lopez. In this procedure a catheter with a tiny balloon at the tip is inserted into a blocked artery and inflated to force the blockage against the wall of the artery. This allows more oxygen-filled blood to flow through the artery to the heart.

Transcribe this letter for Dr. Karns. Punctuate the letter correctly, consulting a reference manual if necessary.

this letter goes to . . . doctor . . . raymond l lewis . . . 2909 lincoln drive . . . waterville . . . ohio . . . 43566 . . . 1004 . . . dear doctor lewis . . . regarding angela lopez . . . date of birth . . . 6 . . . 9 . . . 49 . . . i performed coronary angioplasty on your patient . . . angela lopez . . . an 80 percent lesion in the right coronary was dilated with a 20 percent residual . . . because of the localized dissection . . . stress (capital s) sestamibi (capital s) scanning was performed prior to discharge and was noted to be normal . . . close follow up with you on ongoing risk factor modification was recommended . . . (Paragraph) . . . on behalf of my associates . . . thank you for the opportunity to care for this patient . . . jason karns . . . m d . . .

Type a return visit form, similar to the one shown here, on Unit letterhead. Save it as *return* on your disk.

<u>**RETURN VISIT**</u>

Name   **Weight**   **B.P.**

_____

Date   **H.R.**

_____

Current Meds

_____

_____

_____

_____

_____

_____

JOB 31: Return Visit Report

Use figures and symbols rather than words when typing medical statistics.

Type medical terms and phrases exactly: CO2, 10mm trocar.

Dr. Barnett frequently has referred Stanley Stark to the unit for an evaluation of Mr. Stark's coronary heart disease. A stress MUGA was administered yesterday under the direction of Dr. Szabo. This is a nuclear medicine test to measure ejection fraction of blood.

Complete the report for Dr. Szabo; send Dr. Barnett a copy as well. Use the document *return* for the report. Save this report as *job31*.

Weight: 175 lb
B/P: 140/78
Date:
H.R. 72
Current Meds:
Procardia XL 60 mg q.i.d. Trental. Digoxin 0.125 mg q.i.d. Zantac. Transderm-Nitro. Aspirin grains 5 q.i.d.

The patient was seen to review the results of the stress MUGA test performed at Memorial Hospital on December 7, 1997. The patient reached an exertional level of 5 MET. and 60% of maximum predicted heart rate without symptoms of chest discomfort. There were nondiagnostic changes on EKG. The MUGA scan demonstrated resting left ventricular ejection fraction of 40% with decrease during exercise to 31%.

(continued on next page)

The patient is known to have coronary artery disease with the most recent cardiac catheterization in July 1997, showing total occlusion of the proximal circumflex artery with collateral filling in the distal vessel, 80% stenosis of the midanterior descending artery, and mild disease within the right coronary artery. The previous cardiac catheterization in January 1995 had demonstrated total occlusion of the proximal anterior descending artery with collateral filling in the distal vessel, and thus the lesion identified in July 1997 represented recandulization of an occluded vessel. The patient had undergone coronary angioplasty of 80% lesion in the proximal circumflex artery in January 1995, which then progressed to full occlusion at the time of cardiac catheterization in July 1997. The previous exercise MUGA test in October 1995 had also demonstrated an exertional level of 5 MET. with development of symptoms of chest discomfort. At that time, the resting left ventricular ejection fraction was only 30% and the postexercise ejection fraction was identical to the current study at 31%.

In August 1994 the patient had been admitted to Memorial Hospital with onset of atrial fibrillation. The rhythm converted to sinus following institution of Digoxin. An acute myocardial infarction was excluded during that admission, and a subsequent exercise thallium test performed on August 7, 1994, at Memorial Hospital had demonstrated an exertional level of 5.5 MET. without symptoms of chest pain or definite EKG evidence of myocardial ischemia. The simultaneous thallium scan at that time demonstrated old infarction without definite evidence of exercise-induced ischemia.

In recent months the patient has continued to have occasional symptoms of exertional chest pain, but no symptoms of chest pain at rest, orthopnea, or PND. The patient has noted some improvement in symptoms of dyspnea with exertion in recent months.

It was discussed with the patient that in light of the stability of symptoms, findings on exercise thallium test at Memorial Hospital in August 1994, and unchanged postexercise left ventricular ejection fraction on the current exercise MUGA test compared to the previous study in 1997, there appears to be no definite evidence of progression of coronary disease. The current medications will be continued. The plan will be to continue to perform periodic repeat exercise tests to evaluate for possible evidence of progression of coronary disease. It was also discussed with the patient that if he should have a change in symptoms of exertional chest pain or dyspnea, then consideration will be given for repeat cardiac catheterization to determine if there has been a change in coronary anatomy compared to the previous cardiac catheterization in 1997. The patient will be seen in follow-up by Dr. Eadie and will be seen again in this office for the periodic repeat cardiac evaluation or PRN.

Jeffrey Szabo, M.D.

Remember to type the physician's full name followed by *M.D.* in the inside address. Use *Dr.* and the last name in the salutation.

Dr. Lewis referred his patient Diane Rae to the unit. Dr. Szabo, in turn, performed a cardiac catheterization on Mrs. Rae. In this procedure, a long tube is passed into the heart through a large blood vessel in an arm or leg; by monitoring the tip of the tube, the physician can record the pressure of the flow of blood as it passes the heart.

Dr. Szabo dictated a summary of the operation, which was performed at Memorial Hospital. Type the letter to Dr. Lewis.

this letter goes to . . . doctor . . . raymond l lewis . . . 2909 lincoln drive . . . waterville . . . ohio . . . 43566 . . . 1004 . . . dear doctor lewis . . . regarding diane s rae . . . date of birth . . . 12 . . . 1 . . . 30 . . . enclosed is a copy of the schematic diagram for the cardiac catheterization performed for diane s rae at memorial hospital on march 1 . . . 1997 . . . the catheterization demonstrated essentially normal left ventricular function with possible mild hypokinesis of the inferior wall . . . the coronary angiography demonstrated 70 to 80 percent stenosis of the midright coronary artery and only minor changes within the remaining coronary vessels . . . it appears that the degree of stenosis of the right coronary artery has progressed since the previous cardiac catheterization following inferior myocardial infarction . . . (*Paragraph*) . . . owing to the patients progression of symptoms and the degree of stenosis . . . the plan will be to review the films with doctor eadie for probable early coronary angioplasty of the right coronary artery . . . also . . . the plan will be to continue anticoagulation and monitoring at memorial hospital pending transfer to monroe medical center for coronary angioplasty . . . (*Paragraph*) . . . thank you again for the opportunity to participate in ms raes care . . . if i can provide further information regarding her findings . . . please feel free to call me . . . (*Please add the closing lines, and don't forget to enclose the diagram. Also send a copy of the letter to Dr. Eadie.*)

Is That a Fact?!

To avoid food poisoning, make sure that all meat, poultry, and seafood are completely cooked. You can also prevent it by thoroughly cleaning and disinfecting food preparation areas where raw meat or poultry were handled.

JOB 33: History and Physical Report

Type the headings *admitted, discharged, dictated,* and so forth, in all caps and bold on all report forms. If the discharge date is not provided, omit the date.

Louise Cox was admitted to Memorial Hospital today for unstable angina. Dr. Eadie completed a physical examination of Ms. Cox and received the history of her medical condition.

Type this history and physical report, which was dictated today, on the Memorial Hospital medical record form stored on your data disk as *medrec.* Use Physical Report in the footer.

Physician: Thomas Eadie, M.D.

Room: 491

History No.: 267897

Admitted:

Discharged:

Dictated:

Chief Complaint: Neck and jaw discomfort.

History of the Present Illness: The patient is a 44-year-old female with known premature ischemic heart disease. The patient was recently hospitalized with unstable angina and underwent successful coronary angioplasty of the circumflex anastomotic site of the vein graft to the circumflex. She recently underwent stress thallium testing here at Memorial Hospital. There was a question of both fixed and reversible ischemia involving the inferior segment and an anterolateral fixed defect. The patient has had 2 previous myocardial infarctions involving the right coronary artery and circumflex distribution. She underwent her third bypass operation at the Monroe Clinic with an internal mammary graft to the left anterior descending and a vein graft to the circumflex after her vein graft reoccluded despite emergency PTCA in December of 1996. The patient feels that her anginal symptoms have been worsening, particularly notable when climbing the stairs in the afternoon. She has had relief with nitroglycerin.

Present Medications:
Cardene 20 mg p.o. t.i.d.
Enteric aspirin 325 mg p.o. daily
Zantac
Mevacor 40 mg p.o. b.i.d.

Cardiac Risk Factors: Obesity, severe hyperlipidemia, and smoking. For other details of past noncardiac history, please see chart from July of last year.

Physical Examination: Blood pressure is 128/84 mm of mercury, pulse is 88 and regular, and respirations are 16 and unlabored.

> **General: In general, she is a middle-aged woman, appearing to be her stated age, in no acute distress.**

(continued on next page)

Skin: Without lesions.

Head: Normocephalic, atraumatic.

Eyes: Pupils equal, round, reactive.

Pharynx: Benign.

Neck: Supple. She has no audible bruits. Carotid upstrokes are normal. There is no thyromegaly.

Lungs: Clear and resonant.

Heart: Apical impulse discrete. S1 and S2 are regular in rate and intensity. There is no S3 gallop but there is an S4 gallop. No cardiac murmur.

Abdomen: Obese and nontender. Bowel sounds normoactive. Liver edge is at the costal margin.

Extremities: She does not have any palpable distal pulses. She does have a 2+ popliteal on the left, 1+ on the right, 1+ to trace femoral on the right side, and a 1 to 2+ femoral pulse on the left side.

Neurologic: She has no focal deficits.

EKG reveals evidence of previous inferior, posterior, and lateral myocardial infarctions unchanged from recent tracings.

Laboratory: Sodium 142, potassium 3.7, CO2 29, chloride 103, creatinine 1.1, BUN 13. Her cholesterol remains elevated at 293, CPK 133. Her blood type is A+. Baseline coags returned to baseline now off Coumadin therapy for 2 days. Her hemoglobin was 16.2, hematocrit 49, white count 8,700.

Diagnostic Impressions: Recurrent angina in a setting of known ischemic heart disease, previous PTCA of the circumflex via its bypass graft, and repeat bypass surgery in December of this past year. The PTCA was in July of last year.

Plan: Admit the patient for diagnostic catheterization with possible repeat PTCA should restenosis be identified or other critical focal disease amenable to angioplasty.

Thomas Eadie, M.D.

ma =
milliampere

Following an Emergency Room examination for severe chest pains, Nancy Trumble was admitted today to Memorial Hospital for an emergency cardiac catheterization.

Type this operative report, which was dictated today, on the Memorial Hospital medical records form.

Physician: Jason Karns, M.D.
Room No.: 325
History No.: 289034
Admitted:
Discharged:
Dictated:
Procedure: Emergency cardiac catheterization with left and right coronary angiography, selective injection of vein grafts to the circumflex, left anterior descending, right coronary arteries, intracoronary tissue plasminogen activator, temporary transvenous pacemaker placement, and percutaneous coronary angioplasty of the vein graft to the circumflex.

History and Indications for Procedure: This is a 44-year-old female with known ischemic heart disease, status post coronary bypass operations in 1993 and 1996, who presented to Memorial Hospital Emergency Room with severe chest discomfort described as a 9 to 10 out of 10. She had mild but definite EKG changes and was taken on an emergent basis to the Cardiac Catheterization Laboratory after giving informed consent.

Technique: The right groin was prepped and draped in sterile manner. Local analgesia was applied with subcutaneous infiltration of Xylocaine 2%. Premedication included intravenous Demerol and Valium. A No. 6 French diaphragm sheath was inserted percutaneously into the right femoral artery after difficult negotiation of a highly diseased iliac system. Because of this, all subsequent catheters were exchanged over a guide wire in the descending aorta. The patient was on a heparin drip at the time of her transfer to the Cardiac Catheterization Laboratory; it was not interrupted. Selective left and right coronary angiography was performed with Judkins style 6 French left- and right-tipped, 4-cm catheters with hand injections of Isovue in multiple injections. Selective injection of the bypass grafts to the circumflex, left anterior descending, and previously occluded right coronary bypass were performed utilizing the Judkins JR4 catheter. This did not seat well in the circumflex graft and was exchanged for a modified right Amplatz catheter.

(continued on next page)

A No. 6 French diaphragm sheath was inserted into the right femoral vein for further access prior to the administration of the TPA, and for the need to administer KCL due to hypokalemia. Intracoronary TPA via the vein graft to the circumflex was then administered 20 mg over 10 minutes; it resulted in reperfusion.

The patient was essentially pain-free at the end of the procedure. She was transferred on a heparin drip, 1000 units per hour, to the Coronary Care Unit, where she will be observed.

Jason Karns, M.D.

Portfolio

Choose either the Discharge Summary or the History and Physical Report that you prepared. Correct errors, if any, that you made and resave it as *port3*. Print one copy for your portfolio.

Plastic Surgery

FOCUS ON MEDICAL CAREERS

PATHOLOGIST'S ASSISTANT

*P*athologists' assistants work under the direct supervision of a pathologist. They may work with forensic pathologists who study the human body and diseases for legal purposes, or they may work with anatomic pathologists who study the human body and diseases for research. Pathologists' assistants perform laboratory work that includes studying and photographing microscopic tissue specimens; performing postmortem examinations; and maintaining supplies, instruments, and chemicals for the pathology laboratory.

Pathologists' assistants need to understand the function of organs, tissues, and cells; understand how disease alters normal cell structure and functions; learn about an anatomic pathology laboratory; and learn how to manage a surgical cutting room and an autopsy suite.

Objectives

- Type documents from various kinds of copy: typed, rough draft, handwritten, dictated.
- Create letterhead and memo heading for unit.
- Format and revise one-page and multipage documents used in a plastic surgery office: patient data file, operative consent form, merge letters, letters, authorization for release of medical information.
- Compose a memo.
- Proofread documents; supply necessary capitalization and punctuation; and correct errors.

Terms to Know

ala	dehiscence	hemoglobin	palmar
alveolus	distal	intertrigo	pruritus
areola	fibrocystic	lymphadenectomy	seroma
carcinoma	flexor	melanoma	supraclavicular
carpal	ganglion	metastasis	synovia
cheilorrhaphy	hematoma	nevus	trophic

Today you will begin working in the Plastic Surgery Unit. You will assist Dr. Alvin K. Larson, director; Dr. Janice S. Karns; Mr. Carl E. Omar, chief nurse; and Ms. Louise A. Albert, administrative assistant. Ms. Albert will be your supervisor.

The physicians in the Plastic Surgery Unit specialize in the change, restoration, and replacement of outer body parts in order to correct structural or cosmetic defects. Related surgery is performed at Memorial Hospital. Sites used for testing are the Laboratory and Radiology Departments and the unit testing room.

Document Processing

JOB 35: Plastic Surgery Unit Letterhead

Create a letterhead for the unit, and name it *plaslet*.

JOB 36: Dictated Patient Data Files

> Use a hyphen after a prefix ending in *a* or *i* if the base word begins with the same letter, e.g., *anti-inflammatories*.

Information on patient consultations, routine and follow-up visits, and medical prescriptions is recorded on the Patient Data File. Patients' files are updated each time there is information about the patient to record. These records enable the physician to see the full medical history of a patient provided by that physician or the medical unit over a period of time.

Dr. Karns dictated two notes after examining patients today. Type the notes as Patient Data Files, and use the current date. Save each note as a separate document with the names *job36a* and *job36b*, respectively.

> Since beginning your work at the Center, you have become more familiar with the doctors' dictation and the terminology. Therefore, from this point on, dictated numbers will be presented in words rather than figures. Be sure to type numbers correctly.

(this first note is on kyle longworth) . . . three . . . thirteen . . . sixty one . . . chief complaint . . . numbness . . . tingling . . . and pain in the right hand . . . consultation . . . mister longworth is a thirty eight year old male who works for an auto manufacturer . . . during the last ten months . . . he initially noted some tingling in his fingers then . . . subsequently . . . pain that began to radiate up his right arm . . . the patient uses wrenches and does a repetitive type of work . . . his physician at first placed him in some splints . . . his physician also recommended that mister longworth take time off from his job and undergo physical therapy . . . the patient complied with these recommendations . . . the patient was given motrin and some other antiinflammatories of which he cannot remember the names . . . he states that the splints helped awhile . . . but as soon as he started working again . . . his symptoms got worse . . . at this point . . . even with the splints . . . he still awakens frequently at night and has difficulty getting a good nights rest . . . the patient

(continued on next page)

Type your reference initials and the correct document code on each file.

states that when he drives or when he reads a newspaper . . . his right hand goes to sleep . . . (*Paragraph*) . . . the patient denies any history of diabetes mellitus or thyroid disease . . . he is allergic to penicillin . . . (*Paragraph*) . . . physical examination shows a well developed thirty eight year old male whose right hand shows no trophic changes . . . tinels (*in initial cap with apostrophe s*) and phalens (*apostrophe s*) signs are positive . . . this right handed patient has a good pulse . . . his strength registers two sixty on the right and three hundred on the left . . . (*Paragraph*) . . . the patient brought his emg (*all caps*) and nerve conduction studies that have been carried out by his neurologist . . . these show a definite abnormal study . . . but without evidence of permanent denervation . . . (*Paragraph*) . . . i explained to mister longworth the nature of carpal tunnel . . . i explained to him that in view of his long history and the fact that splints as well as antiinflammatories have not helped . . . it is worthwhile operating . . . the operation and what to expect were explained to him . . . he would wear a splint for a week . . . and the sutures would be removed in two weeks . . . i explained that the wrist incision could remain tender for many months . . . he is to be scheduled for an operation under local anesthesia . . . (*this second note is on william q otto*) . . . five . . . four . . . thirty three . . . chief complaint . . . bleeding lesion of the right temple . . . consultation . . . mister otto is a sixty six year old male who was referred by his family physician because of a lesion that has been bleeding the last several months . . . the patient indicated that he has had this small lesion on his right temple for about a year . . . but he thought very little of it . . . it has grown in size . . . now measuring almost one centimeter in diameter . . . over the last couple of months . . . every time he washes his face and dries it . . . some blood appears on the towel . . . he also has a burning sensation occasionally . . . (*Paragraph*) . . . his past medical history is significant in that he had a myocardial infarct in the past and also has hypertension . . . he is on procardia and . . . on occasion . . . takes nitroglycerin for chest pain . . . he is allergic to erythromycin . . . (*Paragraph*) . . . physical examination shows an umbilicated lesion on the right temple that on vigorous touching bleeds slightly . . . the borders are raised . . . (*Paragraph*) . . . i explained to mister otto that he has a lesion that has the clinical appearance of a basal cell carcinoma . . . i explained to him the nature of the skin cancer . . . the fact that it is locally invasive . . . and that it does not usually metastasize . . . an excision was advised and this could be done under local anesthesia . . . the procedures and what to expect were explained to him . . . all of his questions were answered . . . we agreed to perform the procedure . . .

Is That a Fact?!

Melanoma is a malignant (cancerous) tumor that begins in the cells that produce the skin coloring or pigment. Most malignant melanoma cells are shaded brown or black. Melanoma most often appears on the body of fair-skinned men and on the lower legs of fair-skinned women. Having darkly pigmented skin lowers the risk, but it is not a guarantee against melanoma.

Forms used as legal medical documents are usually formatted on the letterhead of the medical practice.

Both the surgeon and the patient are often asked to sign an operative consent form in order to ensure that both parties clearly understand the conditions of a surgical procedure. Surgeons may also ask the patient for permission to photograph the surgery for medical education, knowledge, or research.

Format the Center's Operative Consent on Center letterhead with double spacing. Make the indicated corrections.

OPERATIVE CONSENT

This is an agreement between Dr. <<PhysicianName>> and myself, <<PatientName>>, ~~reviewing~~ *summarizing* our discussion and knowledge of the conditions under which we consent to ~~begin~~ treatment for <<ChiefComplaint>> scheduled for <<SurgeryDate>>. I understand that Dr. <<PhysicianName>> will use his/her best skill and judgment to attain the desired results, but that the physician cannot, and does not guarantee such results. I further understand ~~also~~ that the physician's ~~outlook~~ *prediction* of the length of time involved, *the* manner of recovery, and possible complications or ~~unwanted~~ *adverse* results ~~are~~ *is* based upon the average response in similar cases. ~~and~~ *I understand* that my response may be different from the usual response.

I ~~leave the final results up to the opinion of~~ *understand that* Dr. <<PhysicianName>>, ~~Whatever (he/she) considers to be~~ *will choose* the best results achievable from a physical or/and artistic viewpoint ~~will be satisfactory to me~~. I promise to cooperat~~ion~~*e* and consent to any method of treatment ~~which~~ *that* seems to have the best chance for success.

~~Payment.~~ I understand that the fee of <<Fee>> agreed upon for the operation covers the surgery and the usual postoperative care rendered by Dr. <<PhysicianName>> and ~~the~~ staff at his/her office and hospital. Regular hospital expenses, laboratory fees, etc. are not included.

I ~~permit~~ authorize Dr. <<PhysicianName>> and such assistants, photographers, and technicians ~~as they~~ he/she may engage for this purpose, to take photographs of me as the physician directs before, during and after ~~the operation.~~ surgery. I also permit such photographs to be published in professional journals and medical books or be used for any purpose ~~which the~~ that my physician may deem necessary in the interest of medical education, knowledge, or research. ~~Authority is further given to permit~~ I permission for the modification or ~~touching up of the~~ and/s publication of these aforementioned photographs and to the publication of information relating to my case, ~~either separately or in connection with the publication of the photographs taken of me. I give permission to~~ If the publication of photographs concerning my case are it is specifically understood that I will not be identified by name.

_____   _____
Patient's Signature   Date

_____   _____
Parent's or Guardian's Signature   Witness's Signature

_____   _____
Surgeon's Signature   Date

JOB 38: Plastic Surgery Unit Memo Heading

Create the unit memo heading, and name it *plasmemo.*

JOB 39: Memo

Dr. Neil Roberts, associate administrator for Medicine, would like you to type this memo regarding the public relations campaign.

To all department*s* and units

Subject: (PR) Campaign

As you *are* aware, the center has been participating in *a* public relations campaign to provide (info) to our patients and the general public about *each of* our units and the highly educated and skilled staff who *work* in those units. This month we *are* focusing on the Dermatology unit.

The <u>Toledo Times</u> is publishing a detailed artica*le* on the unit *in* next Wednesday*'s* edition. Therefore, would you please review the following information before it is released and make any changes or corrections that may be necessary. Please give me *your* ~~any~~ changes by tomorrow noon.

Dr. Clayton Lee Longtree, director of the (H M C) Dermatology Unit, joined the staff (5) years ago. Dr. Susan Meiske-Rose, who worked with Dr. Longtree in Toledo, joined the staff last year. Both ~~of these~~ physicians are alumni of the Ohio College of Medicine. In addition, they were instrumental in the su*c*cess of the greater Toledo area Dermatology Associates. Their association with Dermatology Associates and our Dermatology Unit *has* ~~have~~ resulted in the Center's being recognized and highly respected as a leader in the field of dermatology throughout Northwestern Ohio and Southeastern Michigan. Ms. Justine Harris, the unit's administrative assistant, joined the unit at its *inception* ~~creation~~ almost ten years ago. She (was previously) the office manager of the Good Samaritan Hospital Reconstructive Surgery Department. Her knowledge and experti*s*e has enabled our unit to quickly run *smoothly* ~~quickly~~ and complements the work of our physicians.

The Dermatology Unit is accepting new patients during the Center's scheduled appointment hours. The unit is *located* ~~housed~~ on the third floor in Suites 350-354.

Create a form file, and name it *job40f,* for the form letter that follows. Then, create a data file, and name it *job40d,* to contain the information for the patients listed below. Save the merged letters as *job40a* and *job40b.*

Kyle Longworth, one week from Thursday, as an outpatient.

William Q. Otto, two weeks from Wednesday, as an outpatient.

You have been scheduled for surgery by the Plastic Surgery Unit of Hayes Medical Center on *(date)* as *(an outpatient/a patient)* at Memorial Hospital. *(Insert the last two sentences of paragraph 1 from Job 16.)*
(Insert paragraph 2 from Job 16.)

The second form is an operative consent, which summarizes the discussion and understanding of the conditions under which you and I, as your surgeon, mutually consent to treat your physical ailment or complaint. Please read the form thoroughly, and be prepared to sign it in my presence the day of your surgery.

If you need additional authorization forms for other physicians or have questions concerning your surgery or the operative consent, please call the Center at 419-555-7800.

Sincerely yours,

Janice S. Karns, M.D.

Enclosures

Is That a Fact?!

Lyme disease is a serious infection caused from a bite by a deer tick. The first symptom of Lyme disease is often the appearance of a raised, red dot at the site of the tick bite. In many cases, this bite goes unnoticed. If the condition is diagnosed early, treatment with antibiotics is effective. If left untreated, it can progress to arthritis, heart, and neurological problems.

JOB 41: Authorizations for Release of Medical Information

Update the document code on each document.

Do not replace Job 17 when typing the forms.

Use the form you created in Job 17 to type individual copies of the Authorization for Release of Medical Information for the patients referenced in Job 40. Save the authorizations as *job41a* and *job41b*. On each form add the patient's name and birth date (from the data file), check *All Medical Records*, and provide Dr. Karns's name and address.

JOB 42: Operative Consent

Update the document code on each document.

Do not replace Job 37 when typing the forms.

Dr. Karns would like you to format individual copies of the Operative Consent Form (Job 37) for the patients referenced in Job 40. Using information from the patient data files in Job 36 and the letter in Job 40, type the variable information.

Be sure to include the guardian's name with the name of any minor patient. The surgical fees are as follows: hand pain, $600; bleeding lesion, $500.

Save the documents as *job42a* and *job42b*.

JOB 43: Dictated Patient Data Files

Dr. Karns dictated the following notes after seeing patients in follow-up today. For each patient create a new data file. Refer back to the previous data files in Job 36. Save the documents as *job43a* and *job43b*.

(this is a note on kyle longworth.) ... mister longworth had his operation one and a half weeks ago ... he told me that he has had excellent relief from his symptoms ... he has some tenderness in the wrist at the location of the incision ... he does not wake up any more at night ... and he has no numbness or pain ... i removed the splint ... then i instructed him in active and passive exercises of the wrist and informed him that he can start washing his hand ... i will examine him again in one week ... *(this next note is on william q otto.)* ... william otto had his operation a week ago ... his incision is healing very nicely ... i removed the sutures today and discussed his pathology report with him ... which did show a basal cell carcinoma ... it has been completely excised ... and nothing more needs to be done ... i also have discussed with him that he should try to avoid the sun ... wear a hat in the summer ... and wear some sunscreen ...

JOB 44: Dictated Patient Data Files

Dr. Karns dictated the following notes after examining patients today. Prepare these patient data files, and save them as *job44a* and *job44b*.

(this is a note on kyle longworth.) ... i examined mister longworth today ... his incision is well healed ... he continues to be asymptomatic ... i removed his sutures ... and he is to return in six weeks ... *(the next note is on william otto.)* ... mister otto returned today for a follow-up ... his scar has healed well and is barely visible ... it will continue to mature ... he will be followed by his family physician ... and i will be glad to see him again when necessary ...

JOB 45: Letter

Use a reference manual to verify the correct style of the name of a television series and correct punctuation and spelling.

Ms. Albert typed the following letter for Dr. Larson and then was called into a meeting. She asked you to correct her mistakes as you retype the letter.

William Abbott, M.D.
Tolelo Medical Clinic
4523 Monroe Avenue
Toledod, OH 43605-2400
Dear Bill:
I am hapy to accept your invitation to be a guest panelist on your television series Medical Breakthroughs on Sunday *(full date three weeks from today)*.

As you suggested, I will be happy to discuss plastic surgery and its psychological implications with your distinguished medical panel. the public as well as the medical field should be kept abreast of the turmoil patients facce once they have severely burned or disfigured. We in the plastic surgery unit at Hayes Medical call upon the services of psychologists to assist us in counseling patients before surgery if possible and certainly afterwards if necessary.

As you requested, enclosed is my biographical sketch.
I will be at the WSPD-TV Center on *(same date as above)* at 8:30 a.m., one hour before the program
is to begin. Again, thank you for the opportunity to participate in your award-winning program.
Sincerely yours,
AKL

Portfolio

Revise one of the patient data forms if you have any errors in it. Resave the document as *port4*, and print one copy for your portfolio.

Is That a Fact?!

Diabetes and certain other medical conditions can cause nerve damage. Most often, nerve damage, or neuropathy (nerr-op-ah-thee), affects the feet and legs. Symptoms of nerve damage include loss of feeling, tingling, burning, or pain in the feet and legs, and sometimes the hands. Diabetics must pay special attention to their feet to ensure that they don't become injured or infected.

UNIT 5 Allergy/Immunology

FOCUS ON MEDICAL CAREERS

RESPIRATORY THERAPIST

*R*espiratory therapists, working under the supervision of a physician, diagnose and treat breathing disorders in people who have difficulty breathing. Some patients may have chronic lung problems such as asthma, bronchitis, or emphysema. Others may have difficulty breathing as a result of heart attacks, accidents, cystic fibrosis, or lung cancer.

To diagnose respiratory problems, therapists may analyze patients' breath or blood samples for levels of oxygen, carbon dioxide, and other gases. Therapists may also measure the capacity of patients' lungs to determine if they are working properly.

To treat problems, therapists may use oxygen respirators, oxygen tents, or medication in aerosol form. Therapists may also use mechanical breathing equipment for patients who cannot breathe on their own.

Objectives

- Type documents from various kinds of copy: typed, rough-draft, dictated.
- Create letterhead and memo heading for unit.
- Format and revise one-page and multipage documents used in an allergy/immunology office: release from waiting time after injection(s), consultation report, memos, influenza (flu) vaccine patient consent, radiology report, allergy skin test.
- Compose memos.
- Proofread documents; supply necessary capitalization and punctuation; and correct errors.

Terms to Know

aeroallergens	fiberoptics	inspiratory	postpartum
amoxicillin	flurbiprofen	otalgia	prednisone
antrostomy	gestation	otolaryngologist	pyrethrum
asymmetrical	hyposensitization	paroxysms	rhinoscopy
desensitize	idiopathic	pharyngitis	subarachnoid
empiricism	immunotherapy	pneumococcal	vasomotor

ORIENTATION

Today you will begin working in the Allergy/Immunology Unit. You will be assisting Dr. Andrew Bednar, director; Dr. Shan Chung; and Mildred Tyson, office assistant. Ms. Tyson will supervise your work in the unit.

The doctors in the Allergy/Immunology Unit specialize in the diagnosis and treatment of allergies and deal with the body's resistance to disease. Testing is performed at the Laboratory and Radiology Departments of the Center as well as at Memorial Hospital. Allergy tests are conducted in the unit testing room.

Variations from the Procedures Manual document format guidelines, if any, will be provided with instructions for production jobs.

Ms. Tyson stressed the importance of capitalizing and punctuating documents—especially dictated documents—correctly. Because your familiarity with medical terminology and document processing procedures should be increasing, spelling and style instructions will be limited.

Document Processing

JOB 46: Allergy/Immunology Unit Letterhead

Create a letterhead for the unit, and name it *allerlet.* Use this for all letters and to begin all unit reports and other documents as noted.

JOB 47: Allergy/Immunology Unit Memo Heading

Create a memo heading for the unit, and name it *allermem.*

Is That a Fact?!

A strong whiff of frankincense, lemon, rosemary, or other aromas could be a cure for what ails you. According to its supporters, aromatherapy can reduce appetite, increase energy, calm nerves, boost memory, speed healing, and lower blood pressure. Aromatherapy is the use of scented plant oils that can trigger certain body responses.

Patients must sign a Release from Waiting Time after Injection(s) form. By reading and signing this form, patients become aware of the need to wait in the office after receiving an injection because of the possibility of certain physical or medical changes occurring.

Ms. Tyson edited this draft of the release and would like you to type it in final form.

Type on unit letterhead with single spacing⊙

RELEASE FROM WAITING TIME AFTER INJECTION(S)

I, _____, ~~representing me~~ as legal

guardian to _____, understand the importance *of*

and need ~~of~~ the policy ~~for~~ waiting in the office after each injection.
  the for   regarding   hyposensitization

The members of the office staff have thorough~~told~~ to me the reasons for the
                                              ly explained

required mi~~nim~~um wait of ~~thirty~~ minutes in the office following each
                              30

injection⊙ because of the possibility of severe shock (faint feeling, loss of
  This wait is needed. u/s   i.e.;

consciousness), asthma, or even lethal reaction, and because of ~~importance~~ ~~the~~

of having my arm checked by a~~n~~ staff member at the completion of this
                              office

interval time before I leave.

With this knowledge, should I fail to wait the interval of time after my
                                           prescribed

injection~~s~~ and subsequently exper~~e~~ence an injection reaction, I absolve the
  Allergy/Immunology

~~Unit~~ Hayes Medical Center from related liability.
  and

_____   _____

Patient Signature   Date

WITNESS: _____

JOB 49: Dictated Consultation Letter

Transcribe numbers and abbreviations accurately and in the proper format.

When a date precedes a month or stands alone, it should be presented in ordinal style, e.g., 23d of July, the 1st of the month.

Proofread your finished document. Correctly hyphenate compound adjectives, if necessary. Consult a reference manual if you have questions.

Dr. Katherine Greene had referred her patient, Cassandra Book, to the unit in the past. Dr. Bednar dictated a summary of this year's annual follow-up examination of Ms. Book. Transcribe the report.

this letter goes to doctor katherine greene . . . four six seven main street . . . weston . . . ohio . . . four three five six nine . . . one zero zero one . . . dear doctor greene . . . regarding cassandra book . . . date of birth . . . ten . . . four . . . fifty three . . . miz book had her annual progress examination on the twenty third of july . . . during the past year . . . she has fared exceedingly well on a program that entails starting amoxicillin five hundred milligrams once daily in september and ending in june . . . during that period . . . she gradually weaned herself off allergy injections . . . with the last one given on the fifth of may . . . during the last week of may . . . she took three days of low dose prednisone in order to avoid increasing upper respiratory symptomatology . . . she has been symptom free since . . . (Paragraph) . . . examination of the nasal mucosa was normal . . . (Paragraph) . . . i am advising no change in the program . . . which is to reinstitute use of amoxicillin on a daily basis beginning in the last week of august . . . she is not to return to allergy injection therapy this year . . .

Is That a Fact?!

People working in poorly ventilated offices are more likely to call in sick than people who work in well-ventilated offices are. When the air is continuously recirculated, people are more likely to catch a cold, flu, or other illness from sick co-workers.

JOB 50: Dictated Memo

Dr. Shan Chung has asked you to type the following dictated memo.

memo to . . . all directors . . . subject . . . use of outside laboratory . . . (Paragraph) . . . as you all know . . . our laboratory does not have adequate staff to process all requests in a timely manner . . . therefore . . . after careful study . . . I have decided that biogen laboratories (capital b capital l) will be our outside resource laboratory for the next three months . . . they have contracted to provide us with fast . . . reliable service . . . (Paragraph) . . . biogen is certified to provide all necessary lab work . . . they will bill us directly for any outside services we use . . . also . . . they will send us monthly reports on our use of their services so that we can monitor the cost . . . (Paragraph) if you have any questions . . . please let me know . . .

An influenza vaccine consent form advises patients about the influenza (flu) vaccine, risks involved, and the possibility of physical or medical changes resulting from the injection. A patient must first read and sign the consent form before receiving the influenza vaccine. If a patient is a minor or under the medical care of another individual, the guardian must sign the consent form.

Type the following rough-draft consent form in final form on letterhead. Assume that the second page of the form will be printed on the back of the first page. Type the word *over* in parentheses at the bottom of the first page.

PATIENT ~~INFORMED~~ CONSENT FORM

INFLUENZA (FLU) VACCINE

THE FLU: Influenza (flu) is a respiratory infection caused by viruses. When people get the flu, they may have *symptoms of* fever, chills, headache, dry cough, or muscle aches. Illness may l*a*st several days or a week or more, and complete recover*y* is usual. However, complications ~~may~~ *could* lead to pneumonia or death.

It is not possible to estimate the risk of an ~~individual~~ *person* getting the flu this year. *Nonetheless,* for the elderly and for people with diabetes, *asthma,* or heart, lung or kidney diseases, flu may be especially serious.

THE VACCINE: An injection of flu vaccine will not give you *the* flu, because the vaccine is made from killed viruses. The vaccine is ~~made from~~ *developed* viruses selected by the Office of Biologics, *the* Food and Drug Administration and the Public Health Service.

RISKS AND POSSIBLE REACTIONS: *The* Reactions to influenza vaccine generally are mild in adults and occur at low frequency. These reactions consist of tenderness at the injection site, fever, chills, headaches, or muscular aches. These symptoms *can* last up to ~~forty-eight~~ *48* hours.

A small number of ~~persons~~ *people* who received the 1976 swine flu vaccine suffered a paralysis called Guillain-Barré Syndrome (GBS). GBS is typically characterized by a paralysis that begins in the hands or feet and then moves up the arms or legs or both. GBS is usually self-limiting and most ~~persons~~ *people* with GBS recover without permanent weakness. However, in approximately 5% of the cases, a permanent or even fatal form of paralysis may occur. In 1976, GBS appeared with excess frequency among ~~persons~~ *people* who had received the 1976 swine *flu* vaccine. For ~~the ten~~ *10* weeks following vaccination, the risk of GBS was found to be approximately ~~ten~~ *10*

---

cases for every ~~one~~ **1** million ~~persons~~ **people** vaccinated. This represents a ~~five~~ **5** to ~~six~~ **6** times higher **risk** than ~~in~~ *people would face* unvaccinated ~~persons~~. Younger ~~persons~~ *people* (under ~~twenty-five~~ **25** years *of age*) had a lower risk than others and also had a lower ~~case~~ fatality rate.

¶ Data on the occurrence of GBS have been collected during ~~three~~ **3** influenza seasons since the surveillance began in 1978. These data suggest that, in contrast to the 1976 situation, the risk of GBS in recipients of influenza vaccine was not significantly higher than that in non~~vacciness~~ *recipients*. Nonetheless, ~~persons~~ *people* who receive influenza vaccine should be aware of this possible risk, as compared with the risk of influenza and its complications.

SPECIAL PRECAUTIONS: Children under ~~three~~ **3** years of age have some increased risk of febrile convulsions. Pregnant women should consult with their obstetricians before receiving the vaccine.

¶ ~~Persons~~ *People* who are allergic to eggs or egg products should not receive this vaccine without informing us of such allerg~~y~~ *ies* which may require testing *for tolerance* to the vaccine before it is administered. ¶ ~~Persons~~ *People* with fever should not receive this vaccine. ~~Persons~~ *People* who have received another type of vaccine within the past ~~fourteen~~ **14** days should see their personal physicians before receiving this vaccine.

¶ If you have a reaction *to the injection*, contact a physician immediately. If you have any questions, ~~please ask.~~ *Please let us know before you sign this form.*

CONSENT: I have read the above information and have had an opportunity to ask questions. I understand the benefits and risk**s** of flu vaccination as described *herein*. I request that the vaccine be given to me or the person named below for whom I am authorized to sign.

Information Concerning
Person To Receive Influenza Vaccine

Full Name (Please Print) *use small font*   Date of Birth   Age

---

Address   City   State   ZIP

Signature of person to receive vaccine (or Parent or Guardian)

Witness: _____   Date: _____

JOB 52: Dictated Consultation Letter

Format the subject line, date of birth, and other dates correctly.

As you type, familiarize yourself with special medical terms (*IgE, QIA, IgG4*) so that you will remember their format.

Dr. William Abbott referred his patient, Phil Neuman, to Dr. Bednar for consultation. Transcribe Dr. Bednar's report.

this letter goes to ... doctor william abbott ... toledo medical center ... four five two three monroe avenue ... toledo ... ohio ... four three six zero five ... two four zero zero ... dear doctor abbott ... regarding phil neuman ... date of birth ... six thirty fifty five ... i appreciate the referral of mister neuman ... whom i saw in consultation on the first of (*this month*) ... the present diagnosis is idiopathic perennial rhinitis and a presumptive diagnosis of bronchial asthma ... since december of nineteen ninety-two ... he has had multiple courses of antibiotics for bacterial infection of the paranasal sinuses .... (*Paragraph*) ... the patients occupation since childhood is farming ... in march of nineteen ninety he took a job that exposes him regularly to fossil fuel (*I think that's hyphenated*) combustion products ... he has had symptoms of facial discomfort ... postnasal drainage ... and nasal obstruction on both sides for ten years but progressively worsening over the past two years ... within the past year he has developed symptoms of congestive chest wheeze and breathlessness ... which are consistent with ... but not diagnostic of ... bronchial asthma ... (*Paragraph*) ... physical examination reveals a well developed and well nourished normotensive caucasian male whose external facial features are normal ... he has a superior anterior left nasal septal deflection ... and the nasal mucosa is deep red but not strikingly edematous ... the tonsils were moderate in size ... minimal cobblestoning of the posterior pharynx was noted ... and there is the suggestion of auscultation of the chest for the presence of a low intensity inspiratory (*diagonal*) expiratory wheeze ... the heart was normal ... (*Paragraph*) ... his medical system review indicates that he had a traumatic splenectomy in nineteen ninety one and received pneumococcal vaccine in nineteen ninety five ... he has been subject to recurrent gingival abscesses and dermal furunculosis ... although he has had none of the former for four years and did not have any specific periodontal procedures done to explain their disappearance ... he has not had otitis media ... urinary tract infections ... or chronic diarrhea ... nasal congestion and postnasal drainage failed to improve on beconase (*capital b*) but did improve on nasalide nasal solution (*capital n, n, and s*) ... (*Paragraph*) ... evaluation of pulmonary function revealed a pattern of small airways dysfunction ... the degree of abnormality is not often associated with auscultatory abnormality ... however ... the patients true normals may exceed the predicted ... making the current findings more significant ... the patients allergy skin tests were completely negative other than prick test responses to tomato and green pepper ... (*Paragraph*) ... a dietary history does require looking at tomato ... but not green pepper ... as a possible contributory factor for the patients symptomatology ... however ... i have advised a stricter

(continued on next page)

allergy dietary program . . . which he will begin after he returns from a proposed vacation . . . if dietary management fails to produce results . . . then I feel i g e (*capital i, capital e*) . . . q i a (*all caps*) . . . and quantitative i g g (*capital i and cap the final g*) four studies are indicated . . . if these are normal . . . then the patients choices are surgery . . . topical corticosteroids . . . topical corticosteroids with the use of antibiotic and supplemental oral corticosteroids for a bacterial flareup . . . or topical corticosteroids with prophylactic antibiotic on a daily basis . . . (*Paragraph*) . . . please send me a copy of your evaluation in order that i may confirm the patients opinion that you feel maxillary antrostomies . . . right ethmoidectomy . . . and nasal septal repair are indicated because of the presence of significant inflammatory sinus disease . . .

JOB 53: Allergy Skin Test Form

Nurses and technicians who administer allergy skin tests must record the patients' results on allergy skin test forms. Type this rough-draft allergy skin test form in final form on unit letterhead. If necessary, use double spacing so there is enough space in the table cells to write information.

ALLERGY SKIN TEST (ul)

PATIENT:_____   DATE:_____

DOCTOR:_____   TECH:_____

INFORMED CONSENT SIGNED: YES _____   NO _____

* = Usual Doses				
* Control	P.T.	I.D.		
* Histamine	P.T.	I.D.	+	++
A. Benzylpenicillin 10,000 u/cc				
	P.T.	*10 U/cc	I.D.	10 U/cc
		*100 U/cc		*100 U/cc
		*1,000 U/cc		*10,000 U/cc

		*10000 U/cc		*10000 U/cc

B. Benzylpenicilloate 12000 u/cc (MDM 1 × 10-2M)

	P.T.	*12 U/cc	I.D.	12 U/cc
		*120 U/cc		*120 U/cc
		*1200 U/cc		*1200 U/cc
		*12000 U/cc		*12000 U/cc

C. Pre Pen 6.0 × 10⁻⁵ Benzylpenicilloy[1]

	P.T.		I.D.	

Start new page (handwritten)

(over)) *at bottom of first page* (handwritten)

PATCH TEST: ⟨○⟩ Yes _____   No _____

ABO: _____   Strength: _____

Results: _____

_____

_____

ORAL CHALLENGE

B/P: ____ / ____   Medication: _____

PREVIOUS REACTION: _____

Bold the column heads (handwritten)

Time	Dose	Reaction After 30 Minutes
	mg	
	*2mg	
	10 mg	
	50mg	
	* 250mg	Reaction After 1 Hour

EPHEDRINE AND BENADRYL PILLS GIVEN: YES ____   NO ____

Number the 2nd page at the bottom center. Use only the number. (handwritten)

JOB 54: Revised Consultation Letter

Dr. Bednar read the letter to Dr. Abbott and indicated that paragraphs 3 and 4 should be reversed. Revise Job 52.

JOB 55: Dictated Consultation Letter

Type dates correctly when they are followed by the month, e.g., *1st of December.*

Type T&A with no internal spaces.

Spell-check your work. You may need to refer to a dictionary to verify correct spelling.

Dr. Alex Marsh referred his patient, Albert Cross, for consultation to Dr. Bednar. Dr. Bednar's diagnosis was perennial allergic rhinitis (inflammation of the nose). Type the summary. Albert's date of birth is February 11, 1986.

send this to doctor alex marsh . . . four five six seven telegraph road . . . monroe . . . michigan . . . four eight one six one . . . one zero zero two . . . dear doctor marsh . . . thank you for referring albert cross . . . whom i initially saw in consultation on the first of october . . . his evaluation was completed on the eleventh of november . . . my diagnosis is severe perennial allergic rhinitis . . . at times he has had symptoms of superimposed infection involving both upper and lower airways . . . (*Paragraph*) . . . a history of wheezing is noted . . . occurring at the age of five . . . theophylline sprinkle was prescribed . . . but it was not tolerated . . . a history of bronchospasm induced by exercise or allergen exposure is absent . . . whether albert has asthma or not is an undecided issue . . . t and a at age five appeared to improve episodes of purulent rhinitis . . . a sibling has both asthma and rhinitis . . . alberts medical system review is negative . . . (*Paragraph*) . . . physical examination reveals a normotensive caucasian male in the seventy fifth percentile of weight and the ninetieth percentile of height . . . he has allergic shiners . . . examination of the eardrums by pneumoscopy was normal bilaterally . . . nasal airflow was markedly diminished . . . and the nasal mucosa was pale and wet . . . there was brownish . . . green mucous caked in the nasal vestibules . . . marked cobblestoning and edema of the posterior pharynx were present . . . cervical glands were not enlarged . . . the heart and lung examination was normal . . . (*Paragraph*) . . . allergy skin tests by prick puncture were positive to dust mites . . . cockroach . . . cat . . . dog . . . and ragweed pollen . . . the remainder of comprehensive allergy tests by prick puncture and intradermal were negative . . . (*Paragraph*) . . . in the eight day period between consultation and skin testing . . . the patient showed no further clinical improvement on nasacort nasal inhaler (*capital n, n, and i*) . . . which you had prescribed . . . he showed no increase in the symptomatology when tavist was discontinued before testing . . . there was no improvement on an allergy diet . . . fiber optic rhinoscopy was unsuccessfully carried out on two attempts because of the size of the inferior turbinates and the marked degree of mucous membrane hyperreactivity present . . . this occurred despite preparation for the second exam with three days of prednisone and vancenase a q (*captial v and aq*) nasal spray (*capital n and s*) . . . a brief glimpse of the nasopharynx on the right did not indicate nasopharyngeal obstruction due to adenoidal regrowth . . . although coexisting chronic sinus disease remains a possibility . . . i do not feel it yet

(continued on next page)

appropriate to order c t scans of the sinuses . . . he should continue with intranasal corticosteroid . . . although the size of the anterior tips of the inferior turbinates will prevent significant deposition of the drug posteriorly . . . dust mite control measures were outlined . . . he is consistently exposed to cat at his babysitters . . . and there is no immediate solution for that problem . . . immunotherapy should be given a trial . . . an extract is being prepared for administration under your supervision . . . i would advise no fewer than fifteen days . . . and perhaps twenty-one days . . . on antibiotics for episodes of purulent rhinitis . . .

JOB 56: Memorial Hospital Radiology Report

Begin page 2 at an appropriate point.

Dr. Chung referred Marilyn D. Lopez to the Radiology Department for a CT scan. Type the report using the file *membrad*.

Patient: Marilyn D. Lopez; Med. Rec. No.: 678459; Date of Birth: 4/21/30; Sex: F; Room: OP; Physician: Donald Lincoln, M.D.; Ordering Physician: Shan Chung, M.D.; Date of Exam: (*Yesterday's Date*)

Billing Code: 70486; Billing No.: S14399802; (*Yesterday's Date*); Exam Description: CT Sinuses Noncontrast; Reason: Ethmoid sinusitis.

INDICATION: Ethmoid sinusitis.

CT OF PARANASAL SINUSES: CT examination of the paranasal sinuses was performed utilizing contiguous 3-mm images in their coronal plane. This was performed without intravenous contrast.

There was marked asymmetry of the nasal turbinates with deviation of the nasal septum to the left side. An air fluid level was present in the dependent portion of the right maxillary sinus. Also noted were several soft-tissue densities along the roof, floor, and lateral walls of the maxillary sinus, which would suggest the presence of multiple polyps or retention cysts. There was mucosal thickening along the medial aspect of the left maxillary sinus. Patch ethmoid air-cell consolidation was detected. The left osteomeatal unit was not well defined, suggesting occlusion. The right osteomeatal unit was better defined; however, this also appeared narrowed. The sphenoid sinus appeared unremarkable. There was very minimal mucosal thickening of the right frontal sinus.

The superior aspect of the medial walls of the maxillary sinuses were not well defined. This raised the question of previous surgery, although we were not given a history of previous surgical intervention. Asymmetry and fullness of the turbinates suggested mucosal edema.

(continued on next page)

IMPRESSION:

1. Evidence of mucosal thickening involving the maxillary, ethmoid, and frontal sinuses. There was also suggestion for multiple polyps or retention cysts within the right maxillary sinus.
2. There was a question of previous surgery in this patient, as the superior aspect of medial maxillary walls were not well defined. We were not given a history of previous surgery.
3. The left osteomeatal unit was not well visualized. The right was delineated; however, this appeared markedly narrowed.

/Read By/ Jerome Lawler, D.O., Radiologist Resident

/Released By/ Daniel Lincoln, M.D., Radiologist

JOB 57: Dictated Memo

Dr. Roberts, associate administrator for Medicine, has asked you to type the following dictated memo.

memo to . . . all directors . . . subject . . . publicizing the three new medical units . . . (*Paragraph*) . . . we have spent the last five years seeking permission to add three units to our center . . . oncology . . . surgery . . . and urology . . . six months ago . . . our board of directors . . . the local medical associations . . . the ohio medical association . . . the state of ohio department of health . . . and medical insurance companies approved the addition of the new units . . . (*Paragraph*) . . . since then we have employed staff for the units and have provided space for them within our existing facilities . . . i would like to express my thanks to each of you and your units for assisting in the staffing process of these new units . . . (*Paragraph*) . . . many individuals in the community are now aware of our new units . . . but we must still inform the general public . . . a number of you assisted me five years ago when we added the plastic surgery unit . . . what suggestions do you have for publicizing these new units . . . (*Paragraph*) . . . i will call a meeting with all of you within the next two weeks to develop our promotional strategies . . .

Portfolio

Revise either the Release from Waiting Time After Injections form or the Influenza Vaccine Patient Consent form if you have any errors in them. Resave the document as *port4*, and print one copy for your portfolio.

UNIT 6 Urology

Objectives

- Type documents from various kinds of copy: typed, rough draft, handwritten, dictated.
- Format one-page and multipage documents used in a urology office: patient data file, operative reports, medical instruction forms, consultation reports.
- Create letterhead for unit.
- Extract pertinent information from other data to prepare patient data files.
- Proofread documents; supply necessary capitalization and punctuation; and correct errors.

Terms to Know

aneurysmal	emesis	prostatectomy
avascular	fasciectomy	pyelorenal
catheter	fibrillation	retroperitoneum
collagen	incontinence	sphincter
cystoscopy	invasive	supine
dorsal	occlusion	trabeculated
ectatic	panendoscope	transluminal

ORIENTATION

Today you begin working in the Urology Unit. You will be assisting Dr. Patrick Nehlson, Director of Urology; Dr. Susan Lakota; and Mr. Lou Albertson, Administrative Assistant. Mr. Albertson will be your supervisor.

Doctors of urology specialize in the diagnosis and treatment of diseases of the urogenital system. Minor surgery is performed in the unit's Outpatient Clinic.

Mr. Albertson reminded you that the Procedures Manual remains your first reference in addition to special directions provided with production jobs.

Document Processing

JOB 58: Urology Unit Letterhead

Create the unit letterhead, and name it *urollet.*

JOB 59: Dictated Consultation Letter

Refer to the Procedures Manual for the correct format of a consultation report.

Dr. Nehlson examined Leonard Abrams today to follow up Mr. Abrams's earlier surgery for cancer of the kidney. The letter should be sent to Mr. Abrams's primary physician, Dr. Lyons.

send this letter to . . . doctor jerome k lyons . . . eight thirty seven hubbell street . . . maumee . . . ohio . . . four three five three seven . . . one zero zero two . . . dear jerry . . . regarding . . . leonard abrams . . . date of birth . . . nine . . . twenty . . . sixty one . . . leonard abrams returned today for kidney carcinoma follow up . . . he remains asymptomatic . . . his examination was negative . . . i plan to get his recent blood results through your office . . . and i am extending his follow up period to one year . . . (*Paragraph*) . . . thank you for allowing me to participate in the care of this patient . . . if i can supply you with any more information regarding this patient . . . please feel free to contact me at any time . . .

Is That a Fact?!

Multiple sclerosis is a disease of the central nervous system. Its effects can range from minor physical annoyances to major disabilities. MS occurs when the protective sheath that insulates nerves becomes inflamed or destroyed. Some consequences of this disease are loss of muscular coordination, impaired vision, and incontinence.

Refer to the Procedures Manual for the correct format of an operative report.

Proofread your finished document.

Dr. Patrick Nehlson's patient, James J. Church, was admitted to Memorial Hospital today for a cystoscopy and periurethral collagen injection. In this procedure a viewing device is used to view the urethra, and collagen (a bundle of small fibers which form connective tissue) is placed in the bladder.

Type the report, dictated today, on the Memorial Hospital medical records form.

Room No. 890

History No. 10056

ADMITTED: (Current Date)

DISCHARGED: (Current Date)

DICTATED:

PREOP DIAGNOSIS: Stress urinary incontinence, post radical prostatectomy.

POSTOP DIAGNOSIS: Same.

OPERATION: Cystoscopy and periurethral collagen injection.

ANESTHESIA: General.

HISTORY: This is a 56-year-old white male who underwent radical retropubic prostatectomy approximately three years ago and became totally incontinent postop. He has had previous periurethral collagen injections and has returned for an additional injection. After the last collagen injection he was totally dry, but then became wet again.

OPERATIVE FINDINGS: Residual collagen was revealed on the left side of the bladder neck.

PROCEDURE: The patient was given general anesthesia and prepped and draped in the usual sterile manner in the dorsal lithotomy position. A #22 panendoscope was passed under video control into the bladder. The findings are described above. A total of 8 cc of collagen was then injected in the distal membranous urethra and sphincter area, and more occlusion of the urethra was noted. The bladder was emptied and the patient was sent to the recovery room in satisfactory condition.

Read the entire form before you begin to type.

Dr. Lakota, in conjunction with the nursing staff at Memorial Hospital, developed the following postoperative instructions for extracorporeal shockwave lithotripsy patients. In extracorporeal shockwave lithotripsy procedure, kidney stones are crushed through the use of high-intensive shockwaves, without open surgery of the kidneys. The procedure is usually completed in an outpatient setting.

Type the form single spaced on Unit letterhead.

<u>Postoperative Instructions For The Extracorporeal Shockwave Lithotripsy Patient</u>   *Underline the title*

1. Call our office for a follow-up appointment if you do not already have one.

2. ~~You may~~ expect some burning on urination, blood-tinged urine, and urinary frequency; this should NOT persist beyond 24–48 hours.

3. You will probably be stiff or have sore muscles for a day or two following your treatment.

4. Drink ~~more~~ extra fluids to help pass the pieces of stones. ~~You should~~ drink 3–4 liters fluid each day. Drink ~~1-2 pints~~ usually of ~~water~~ MORE than you ~~drink~~ during a ~~usual~~ normal day.

5. ~~It is possible that~~ you ~~can~~ may have symptoms similar to passing a kidney stone for a day or two after your treatment. This can includes pain in your side near the kidney area, with pain shifting to the groin area, ~~This~~ which results from the passing of your stones. It is important that you help FLUSH the pieces of stone by drinking large amounts of fluids. If the symptoms become worse, call our office or go to the Emergency Department at ~~the~~ Memorial Hospital.

6. You will be given a strainer for your urine. ~~It is important to~~ strain all urine ~~and~~ to collect all the pieces of stones ~~and~~ give them to your doctor, who ~~You may be~~ given you ideas to prevent more stones.

7. You may have some bruising of the skin at the treatment site. If this area remains swollen with no decrease in pain for ~~36~~ 72 hours, contact our office.

8. Please notify our office if any of the following symptoms occur:
   • Burning upon urination lasting more than ~~24~~ 48 hours.
   • Increasing pain in the kidney area or side of your back that was treated.
   • Bright red bleeding with or without clots after ~~three~~ (3) days.
   • Inability to urinate.
   • Fever ~~of~~ over 101° ~~degrees~~.

Dr. Newton wrote the following operative report today. In this procedure the prostate gland was removed and collagen was inserted in the bladder.

Type the report on the form *medrec*, and send a copy of it to Dr. Nehlson.

Patient: Lucas K. Sawaia

Room No.: 444

History No.: 1058

Admitted: (Current Date)

Discharged:

Dictated:

Preop Diagnosis: Stress urinary incontinence secondary to radical prostatectomy.

Postop Diagnosis: Same.

Operation: Cystoscopy with periurethral collagen injection.

Anesthesia: General anesthesia.

History: The patient is a 59-year-old white male who underwent a retropubic prostatectomy and is now here for his 6th periurethral collagen injection. He has had approximately 90% improvement of his continence with the collagen.

Operative Findings: Open bladder neck with scarring in the membranous urethra and the sphincter is open. There is evidence of previous collagen injection at the level of the sphincter.

Procedure: The patient was given general anesthesia and prepped and draped in the usual sterile manner in the dorsal lithotomy position. Under video control the panendoscope was passed into the bladder. The findings were as described above. A total of 18 cc of collagen was then injected at the level of the sphincter and the resection occlusion noted. A 16 straight catheter was then passed to drain the urinary bladder and the patient was sent to the recovery room in satisfactory condition.

Mr. Albertson wants you to type the following rough-draft copy of the new prostate biopsy form on Unit letterhead.

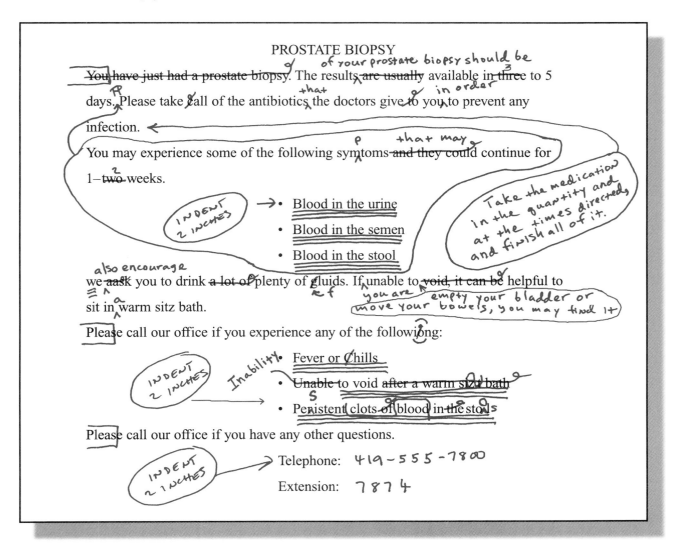

Dr. Alice Conklin, of Hillsdale, Michigan, referred Joseph L. Vargas to Dr. Nehlson for a second opinion regarding the diagnosis of prostate cancer. Transcribe the letter of Dr. Nehlson's findings and his proposed treatment.

this letter goes to doctor alice conklin ... four three five michigan avenue ... hillsdale ... michigan ... four nine two four two ... three two one two ... dear doctor conklin ... regarding ... joseph l vargas ... date of birth ... september twentieth ... nineteen forty five ... mister vargas is a fifty four year old male seen because of recently diagnosed prostate cancer ... three years ago ... he had a psa ... *(all caps)* ... of seven point one ... an ultrasound was suggested ... but the patient did not have it performed ... his brother has a history of prostate cancer and had previous radiation therapy followed by a salvage cystoprostatectomy and orthotopic neobladder ... *(Paragraph)* ... approximately two years ago ... in may nineteen ninety seven ... mister vargas had a psa ... *(all caps)* ... of fifteen point seven ... and ultrasound revealed a two point five centimeter hypoechoic area that was biopsied and showed a gleason ... *(capital g)* ... score of seven carcinoma ... perineural invasion was noted on the right side involving fifty percent of the tissue ... with a gleason score of seven carcinoma ... on the left side ... the biopsy also showed seventy percent of the core involved for a gleason score of seven ... the patient has been cared for by you ... and a radical prostatectomy was advised ... and he was given a three month depot ... *(capital d)* ... shot of lupron ... *(capital l)* ... on may ninth ... nineteen ninety eight ... bone scan was negative with arthritic changes in l *(capital el)* five ... he had no significant urinary symptoms prior to the diagnosis ... and there has not been any appreciable change since being on the endocrine therapy ... medications include hytrin ... *(capital h)* ... ativan ... *(capital a)* ... and lupron ... *(capital l)* ... he has had adverse reactions in the past to sulfa and betadine ... *(capital b)* ... *(Paragraph)* ... previous surgery includes a fibroid tumor in the small bowel and later a small bowel obstruction ... he also has a history of hypertension ... no cigarette or alcohol use is noted ... family history is significant in that both his father and brother have had prostate cancer ... *(Paragraph)* ... physical exam ... abdomen shows no mass ... penis and testicles are normal ... rectal exam shows a fifteen to twenty gram prostate that is symmetrical without nodularity or induration ... *(Paragraph)* ... impression ... carcinoma of the prostate ... clinical stage ... *(capital t)* ... two ... small c ... capital n ... small x ... capital m ... small o ... *(Paragraph)* ... studies ordered ... outside slides submitted today for review ... *(Paragraph)* ... treatment ... treatment options were reviewed at length with the patient and his wife ... and they were given written information on all of the options and complications ... the options discussed included observation ... surgery ... radiation therapy ... and alternate treatments such as implant radiation and cryosurgery ... he would clearly not be suited for observation ... my bias would be toward a radical prostatectomy ... he was advised that consultation with a

(continued on next page)

radiation oncologist would be very reasonable ... the patient is interested in possibly receiving another shot of lupron and delaying the treatment for another three months ... and i do not think there is any risk associated with this ... it is possible he could have a nerve sparing dissection done on one side ... but that may not be feasible because of the disease and because of his hormonal therapy ... the risks of incontinence were discussed in detail ...

JOB 65: Patient Data File

Dr. Nehlson would like you to type a patient data file for Joseph L. Vargas. Extract the chief complaint and consultation information from Dr. Nehlson's letter to Dr. Conklin (Job 64).

Portfolio

Revise the Postoperative Instructions for the Extracorporeal Shock-wave Lithotripsy Patient form if you have any errors in it. Resave it as *port6*, and print one copy for your portfolio.

Is That a Fact?!

Several million Americans experience urinary incontinence, which is the involuntary release of urine. Although it can affect people of all ages, it is most common in older people. Incontinence can be caused by reduced muscle strength, stress, enlarged prostate gland, childbirth, nerve damage, and excess weight.

FOCUS ON MEDICAL CAREERS

CYTOTECHNOLOGIST

Cytotechnologists examine human cells under a microscope to look for indications of disease. Cytotechnologists assist physicians in obtaining and preparing specimens. They stain the specimens with special dyes to see more easily any abnormalities in the cells. The cells come from pap smears, sputum, urine, cerebrospinal fluid, other body cavity fluids, fine needle aspirates, and other sources. Cytotechnologists also perform a variety of specialized tests to identify specific kinds of tumors.

Cytotechnologists must sit at a microscope and concentrate for long periods of time. They need to have fairly good eyesight in order to pick out fine details in cells under the microscope. They usually work in the pathology department under the medical direction of a pathologist in hospitals, private laboratories, or universities.

Objectives

- Type documents from various kinds of copy: typed, rough draft, handwritten, dictated.
- Format and revise one-page and multipage documents used in a surgery office: consultation report, memo, operative reports, patient data file, medical information form, form letter, laboratory report.
- Create letterhead and memo headings for unit.
- Prepare patient data files.
- Proofread documents; supply necessary capitalization and punctuation; and correct errors.

Terms to Know

adenopathy	hepatosplenomegaly	lesions
auscultation	hypertrophic	lipomas
cholecystectomy	intraperitoneal	malleoli
enterotomies	laparoscopic	palpation
femur	laparotomy	pneumoperitoneum
fibroperitoneal	laxity	trocars
hemostasis		

ORIENTATION

Today you will begin working in the Surgery Unit. You will be assisting Dr. Milton Patterson, Director; Dr. Mildred Phelps; Ms. Christine Lay, R.N.; Ms. Mildred Wheeler, R.N.; and Ms. Jean Glazer, administrative assistant. Your supervisor will be Ms. Glazer.

The surgeons are concerned with diseases and injuries that require an operation. Other physicians in the Center assist the surgeons when they need specialists. The unit is noted for knee replacements. Major surgery is performed at Memorial Hospital. Tests are done in the Laboratory and the Radiology Department. Some outpatient surgery is performed within the unit.

Ms. Glazer would like you to review the Procedures Manual when questions arise.

Document Processing

JOB 66: Surgery Unit Letterhead

Create the unit letterhead, and name it *surglet*.

JOB 67: Dictated Consultation Letter

Use parentheses to enclose numbers of an enumeration within a sentence.

Dr. Feigleson referred his patient, Ms. Frances L. Shoemaker, to Dr. Patterson. Ms. Shoemaker complained about her arthritis and right knee. Arthritis is a common ailment that consists of swelling and pain in joints of the body. Dr. Patterson dictated this consultation report for you to transcribe.

Read the entire report before you begin to type.

Hyphenate *58-year-old* because it functions as an adjective before the noun.

Capitalize the first letter in medications, e.g., DiaBeta.

Type *D&C* in all caps with no spaces between.

Use parentheses to enclose numbers of an enumeration within a sentence.

send this to doctor harry . . . g . . . feigleson . . . three fifty six . . . south main street . . . bowling green . . . ohio . . . four three four zero two . . . one zero one one . . . dear doctor feigleson . . . regarding . . . frances . . . el . . . shoemaker . . . date of birth . . . four . . . twenty one . . . forty one . . . miz shoemaker was seen in consultation today concerning increasing problems she has been having with both lower extremities . . . but primarily her left knee . . . she is a fifty eight year old woman who recognizes that she is overweight . . . she works as a secretary at bowling green state university . . . where she has been employed for thirty two years . . . (*Paragraph*) . . . she reports that . . . as best she can remember . . . her knee problems started with the right knee that she hit on a desk about five years ago . . . which resulted in an arthroscopic procedure to the right knee . . . it has improved . . . but it has shown some progressive evidence of deterioration with a lateral migration . . . the left knee was treated with an arthroscopic procedure for torn cartilage by doctor lewis three years ago . . . it has not consistently improved . . . and miz shoemaker has had intermittent aching . . . these findings . . . associated with flat feet and bunion formation . . . have

(continued on next page)

contributed to her present level of disability ... (*Paragraph*) ... she has sleep interference one or two nights per week ... the left knee bothers her the most ... next are the feet and ankles ... then her right knee ... she avoids stairs when possible ... she finds that any prolonged standing is limited ... and that she has now had to give up walking for pleasure or exercise ... she is at a point where she requires help with her foot hygiene ... (*Paragraph*) ... her general health is affected by diabetes ... which is controlled with diabeta ... (*capital d and capital b*) ... and by shortness of breath with exertion ... her family history includes heart disease ... diabetes ... and obesity ... and she has a sister with serious asthma ... the only other medication she lists is oruvail (*capital o*) ... which is becoming less and less effective for her arthritis ... (*Paragraph*) ... she has had previous operations including appendectomy ... hysterectomy ... tonsillectomy ... d and c (*capital d and capital c*) ... and bladder suspension ... (*Paragraph*) ... on physical examination she is notably overweight at two hundred fifty one pounds ... her current height is five feet five and a half inches ... she is able to get in and out of a chair independently utilizing the arm rests ... she hesitates to initiate motion and ambulates with bilateral flat feet and valgus alignment of the right knee ... measuring nine inches between her medial malleoli with her knees touching ... primarily because of the left knee and bilateral ankle valgus ... the overall contour of the feet is not remarkable with the exception of bilateral hallux valgus with bunion formation ... the pronated flat feet are believed to be compensatory ... as maximum dorsiflexion with the foot in neutral is minus ten degrees ... indicating short heel cords ... (*Paragraph*) ... the range of motion of both knees is actually quite good ... from zero to one hundred twenty degrees ... with a slight reversal of the usual valgus alignment on the left to neutral ... there is severe medial and lateral joint line tenderness and crepitus ... there is patellar crepitus ... but this does not elicit significant discomfort ... (*Paragraph*) ... on the right ... the valgus measures twenty degrees ... again with severe medial and lateral joint line tenderness and crepitus ... however ... the left knee is the more symptomatic of the two ... she demonstrates a good range of motion of both hips ... flexing well past ninety degrees ... with twenty degrees internal and forty degrees external rotation without symptoms ... she reports that she has had constant . .. intermittent ... chronic low back pain ... and demonstrates tenderness over the el four hyphen five and el five hyphen s one interspaces which is not referred ... (*Paragraph*) ... a review of x rays that she brought with her ... which are believed to be from wood county hospital ... dated september twenty seven ... nineteen ninety eight ... shows fairly well maintained joint spaces with a measured twenty degree valgus on the right and a four degree alignment on the left ... these films were compared with those taken in the office today ... todays films are single weight bearing films showing total and complete loss of the joint space laterally with bone eroding against bone and

(continued on next page)

generous hypertrophic bony spur proliferation at the margin of the films . . .
there is a compensatory opening of the medial compartment . . . and additional
spur proliferation along the articular margin . . . (*Paragraph*) . . . the findings on
the left show medial joint line narrowing with a deficit along the medial
femoral condyle and bony spur proliferation . . . there is evidence of
patellofemoral arthrosis as well . . . there is a tibial bow at or slightly above the
mid shaft level bilaterally . . . (*Paragraph*) . . . in summary . . . the patients history
. . . physical findings . . . and x ray findings are compatible with advanced
degenerative arthritic changes of the right knee and early to moderately
advanced degenerative arthritic changes of the left knee . . . particularly in the
medial compartment on the left . . . this is superimposed over compensatory
flat feet deformities with bunion formation bilaterally . . . (*Paragraph*) . . . in
regard to the knees . . . we discussed the following alternatives . . . one . . . do
nothing . . . two . . . continue with anti inflammatory medications and or assist
devices as may be appropriate . . . three . . . assessment for arthroscopic
evaluation . . . four . . . total knee joint replacement . . . and . . . five . . . fusion or
angulation osteotomy which were mentioned only in passing as they are not
felt to be realistic alternatives . . . (*Paragraph*) . . . regardless of the pathway
followed . . . a renewed commitment to slow . . . gradual weight reduction will
be an important part of any treatment . . . (*Paragraph*) . . . for the left knee . . .
since the determination of the medial compartment cartilage status is less
definitive . . . assessment for repeat arthroscopy would seem wise . . .
(*Paragraph*) . . . when her symptoms are sufficient to require operative
intervention . . . total knee arthroplasty replacement would give her the most
positive results . . . because of the pseudolaxity of the medial collateral
ligament . . . an articulated prosthesis . . . in my opinion . . . would be the
selection of choice . . . (*Paragraph*) . . . her compensatory bilateral flat feet and
bunion formation would best be treated by an orthopedist who specializes in
foot care . . . i would suggest doctor linen . . . in detroit . . . in the meantime . . .
the role of anti inflammatory medications would best be managed in your
hands . . . (*Paragraph*) . . . should she reach a point where additional
consideration for joint replacement is necessary . . . i would be happy to see her
. . . at that time we would discuss the possible risks and complications
associated with total joint replacement . . . including
possible death from anesthetic or thromboembolic
phenomena . . . failure of healing . . . loosening . . .
breakage . . . or dislocation of component parts . . .
infection . . . neurovascular complications . . . and possible
leg length discrepancies . . . complications with blood
component replacements would also be discussed . . .
including aids (*all caps*) and hepatitis . . . (*Paragraph*) . . .
thank you for the opportunity to see and care for miz
shoemaker . . .

Is That a Fact?!

New surgical instruments are no wider than
a pencil tip. Surgeons use these smaller
instruments to remove gallbladders and
perform other abdominal operations. These
instruments produce smaller scars and
reduce patients' recovery time.

Type the paragraph headings *admitted*, *discharged*, and *dictated* in all caps on all operative reports. If the discharge date is not provided, omit the date.

Use figures and symbols rather than words when typing medical statistics.

Type medical terms and phrases exactly: CO2, 10 mm trocar.

Dr. Mildred Phelps performed a laparoscopic cholecystectomy on Pamela C. Haggerty today. In laparoscopic cholecystectomy surgery, an instrument with a lighted tube and magnifying lenses is inserted into the abdomen to view the abdominal cavity and to assist in the removal of the gallbladder. The patient was admitted today, in Room 345, with history number 10060. Type a final copy of this rough-draft operative report on the form *Medrec*.

PREOP DIAGNOSIS: Cholelithiasis.

POSTOP DIAGNOSIS: Same.

PROCEDURE: Laparoscopic cholecystectomy.

ANESTHESIA: General endotracheal.

PROCEDURE: The patient was brought to in the operating room and placed on the table in a supine position. After induction of general endotracheal anesthesia, a foley catheter was placed and the abdomen prepped and draped sterilely. The patient was placed in trendelenburg's position. A small incision was made at the umbilicus. The abdominal wall was grasped and elevated with sharp towel clips. A veress needle was passed into the abdomen. Clear intraperitoneal position was confirmed by aspiration and inflow of saline with the drop test. The abdomen was inflated with co2. Low insufflation pressures were present. When satisfactory pneumoperitoneum was achieved, the veress needle was removed and a 10 mm trocar passed at the umbilical site. Intraperitoneal position was confirmed with the video laparoscope. No evidence of bowel injury or bleeding was present. The upper abdomen was then visualized and the patient was placed in reverse trendelenburg's position. Two 5 mm trocars were passed in the right subcostal area. These sites were passed under direct vision. The 5 mm sites were used for grasping forceps which manipulated and retracted the gallbladder. A 10 mm trocar was passed in the upper mid line position. This site was also passed under direct

(continued on next page)

vision. The 10 mm site was used for dissection, clip application,
electrocautery, etc. The fundus of the gallbladder was then grasped
and elevated towards the right shoulder. The infundibular region was
also grasped and placed on traction. Calot's triangle was dissected
bluntly. The fibroperitoneal tissue in this area was spread and
striped towards the common duct. Using this technique, the cystic
duct and artery were clearly identified. These structures were
followed onto the gallbladder. The common duct was visualized
through the peritoneum and was well away from the area of
dissection. The cystic duct and artery were then controlled with
clips and divided. The posterior vascular branch was also clipped
and divided. The gallbladder was freed from it's bed using blunt
technique and the electrocautery unit. Prior to dividing the last
attachments to the gallbladder, the intrahepatic region was irrigated
and examined. No active bleeding or other abnormalities were
present. The final attachments to the gallbladder were divided and
the gallbladder removed through the upper 10 mm trocar site. The
trocar was replaced, and the perihepatic region again irrigated and
examined. No active bleeding or other abnormalities were present.
The pneumoperitoneum was evacuated and the trocar removed. The
skin was then closed with 3-0 Vicryl subcuticular sutures. Steri-
strips and dressing were applied and the patient was taken to the
recovery room in stable condition.

Is That a Fact?!

Tai Chi, a centuries-old martial art that emphasizes balance and body awareness, can help older people reduce the likelihood of falls. It can also boost their confidence in their physical abilities. Older people taking Tai Chi suffer fewer falls and have less fear of falling. They also have lower blood pressure after exercising.

JOB 69: Knee Replacement Guidelines

Read the entire form before you begin to type.

Ms. Wheeler, with the assistance of the staff, has developed a set of guidelines for patients who have had knee replacements. She has asked that you type the guidelines on unit letterhead. The last portion is still handwritten.

Guidelines for Returning to Activity After Total Knee Joint Replacement

Immediate

After total knee joint replacement, unless otherwise instructed, the patient may start walking and bearing full weight on the operated extremity the next day, using a walker, crutches, or a cane for balance and security.

Intermediate (one month)

As strength and balance improve, individuals may return to reasonable unlimited walking as desired, and wean themselves from assistive devices when they feel safe and secure, usually between two weeks and three months. They may return to driving, if appropriate, when they decide they can do so safely.

Late (after three months)

Many people are able to return to activities that include gardening, lawn mowing, light work, golfing, bowling, slow dancing, swimming, and riding an exercycle without resistance or a bicycle. People may also do limited hiking, hunting, and fishing, if they use common sense and their general health is good.

Persistent tenderness and limited range of motion in flexion after knee replacement does not usually allow people to kneel or squat. Some swelling and warmth are expected to continue for several months. Numbness next to the incision is expected to improve slowly, but rarely returns to "totally normal." Discomfort tends to diminish as range of motion and strength improve, sometimes taking up to a year or more.

Thigh muscle strength helps to protect the knee from "giving way," injury, and pain. Continuation of thigh muscle exercises as instructed is recommended indefinitely.

It is not advisable to attempt activities such as running, jumping, contact sports, hard physical labor, or working at unprotected heights.

Dr. Patterson dictated this short letter to Frances Shoemaker concerning his evaluation and alternative treatments of her knee complaint. Type this on letterhead and enclose a copy of Dr. Patterson's consultation letter to Dr. Feigleson (Job 67).

> this letter goes to . . . miz frances . . . el . . . shoemaker . . . you can find her address in her file . . . dear miz shoemaker . . . (*Paragraph*) . . . i am pleased to have had the opportunity to see you in my office and evaluate your condition . . . (*Paragraph*) . . . enclosed is a summary of the evaluation and alternatives we discussed . . . (*Paragraph*) . . . i am sure this information will assist you in making a decision about the medical treatment you want to pursue in relation to your knee . . .

JOB 71: Memorial Hospital Operative Report

Read the entire report before you begin to type.

Bruce Erickson decided to have his lipomas removed. Dr. Phelps completed the following operative report. The patient was admitted today, in room 788, and with history number 10061. Type the report with a copy to Dr. Larry Williams.

PREOP DIAGNOSIS: Multiple lipomas of chest, right flank, and right thigh.
POSTOP DIAGNOSIS: Same.
OPERATION: Excision of multiple lipomas of chest, right flank, and right thigh; excision of right thigh skin lesion.
ANESTHESIA: Local with intravenous Versed sedation.
OPERATIVE FINDINGS: The patient was found to have lipomatous-like lesions as described with 3 lipomas excised from the right chest, 2 adjacent ones excised from the right flank, and a large, more adherent lipoma excised from the right medial thigh. The lesions were sent as separate specimens to pathology. A small, darkly pigmented skin lesion immediately adjacent to the right thigh lipoma site was also excised and sent as a specimen to pathology. This was with the patient's consent given at the time of surgery.
PROCEDURE: The patient was taken to the operating room and placed on the operating table in supine position. The patient's chest area and leg were shaved, and they were sterilely prepped using Betadine scrub solution. The right thigh was then prepped using Betadine solution. The skin was anesthetized over the lesion using 1% Xylocaine solution with Epinephrine. A skin incision was then made longitudinally over the lipoma using a No. 15 scalpel. The incision was carried down through subcutaneous tissue using bovie electrocautery and blunt dissection using hemostat. An underlying large lipomatous mass was located which was densely adherent to the surrounding tissue. This was carefully freed using blunt and sharp dissection with Metzenbaum scissors and hemostat. The lipoma was adherent to the underlying muscular fascia, and a small portion of

(continued on next page)

the fascia was taken with the lipoma. The lipoma was passed from the field and sent as a specimen. The area was carefully dried using bovie electrocautery on any small bleeding vessels. Immediately below the incision a pigmented skin lesion was noted, and this was excised in continuity with the incision using a small ellipse of skin around the skin lesion, with the incision made using a No. 15 scalpel blade. The specimen was passed as a separate specimen to pathology. The skin area was dried using bovie electrocautery. The wound was then closed using 3-0 Vicryl suture in buried interrupted fashion to close the subcutaneous tissue and deep dermis. The skin was then closed using 4-0 Monocryl suture in a running subcuticular fashion. Half-inch Steri-Strips were applied transversely across the incision. The drapes were then removed and the chest and flank area were widely prepped using Betadine solution and draped. The skin incisions to be made over lipomas were marked on the skin using a surgical skin marker. The skin was then anesthetized over the 3 chest lipoma sites using 1% Xylocaine solution with Epinephrine. All 3 lesions were removed using separate transverse skin incisions made using a No. 15 scalpel. The blunt dissection was then done using a hemostat. Ability to squeeze the lipomas out using pressure on the margins was achieved with the base of the lipomas removed from the surrounding tissue using bovie electrocautery. The lipomas were sent to the lab as separate specimens marked right chest lipoma, mid chest lipoma, and left chest lipoma. The wounds were then dried using bovie electrocautery and, after good hemostasis was achieved, were closed using 3-0 Vicryl suture in buried interrupted fashion to close the subcutaneous tissue and deep dermis. The skin was closed using 4-0 Monocryl suture in a buried interrupted fashion.

Attention was then turned to the right flank area where the skin was anesthetized using 1% Xylocaine solution with Epinephrine. A transverse incision was made over the lipoma using a No. 15 scalpel. Dissection of the skin was carried out using hemostat for blunt dissection. Initial lipoma was then squeezed out from the wound and freed from the surrounding tissues using bovie electrocautery and was passed from the field and sent as a specimen to pathology. An additional, small lipoma was noted located adjacent to this, which was also squeezed out. This was a separate lipoma located immediately adjacent to the first lipoma, and this was also removed using bovie electrocautery to divide any small adherent strands of tissue. These lipomas were sent to the lab together as right flank lipomas. After noting good hemostasis, the wound was closed using 3-0 Vicryl suture to close the subcutaneous tissue and deep dermis. The skin was closed using 4-0 Monocryl suture in a simple interrupted subcuticular fashion. Half-inch Steri-Strips were then applied across the 3 chest incisions and the right flank incision, and the area was then covered using 4 x 4 gauze secured in place using 3M Medipore Tape. The patient tolerated the procedure well without any known complications. All counts were correct at the end of the procedure. The patient was then taken to the outpatient area and will be discharged home today. He will follow-up in my office in approximately 6 days.
c: Larry Williams, M.D.

Drs. Patterson and Phelps, with the assistance of the nursing staff, developed the following form letter to be sent to all patients who elected to have total knee replacement. Type the letter on unit letterhead.

Dear Patient:

Your decision to proceed with total knee replacement is a good one. The operation will relieve your pain and should improve your level of mobility.

Post-operative needs of patients with knee replacements vary greatly. Healthy, young individuals may require just a few therapy sessions after knee surgery to become completely independent. Older individuals with no family or friends to help them at home or with homes that are difficult to navigate may need special equipment to aid mobility. Some individuals may benefit from a short stay in a rehabilitation facility or a foster care home. To speed your recovery, you should identify and address any special needs before your operation.

To help you fully recover, we have developed a coordinated pathway of physical and occupational therapy for your evaluation and guidance through ARM, a fully licensed and approved rehabilitation and therapy service. We recommend that you follow a pathway of at least one visit or interview before your operation to:

1. **Determine your needs for special equipment for ambulation, dressing, self-care, and bathroom independence.**
2. **Learn correct techniques for getting in and out of bed, automobiles, and the shower; sitting and getting up from a seat; and going up and down stairs.**
3. **Learn what exercises will help facilitate your recovery.**

The goal for your knee is to: straighten, bend past 90° on flexion, provide strength and stability to hold you up safely, and not hurt (unfortunately, this usually comes last and may take several months).

Achieving these goals usually requires two to three therapy sessions each week for one to three weeks, and sometimes longer.

Is That a Fact?!

Hip replacement surgery is now performed on many adults under the age of 65. Most of these people remain physically active for many years afterward. Medical advances such as cementless joints into which bones can grow have made this possible.

JOB 73: Surgery Unit Memo Heading

Create a memo heading for the unit, and name it *surmemo*.

JOB 74: Dictated Memo

Dr. Alvin K. Larson, Director, Plastic Surgery, was asked to assist Dr. Phelps with further surgery on Bruce Erickson. After visiting with Mr. Erickson, Dr. Larson dictated the following memo as a consultation report to Dr. Phelps. Type the memo on the Plastic Surgery Unit's memo form.

this memo goes to mildred phelps . . . m d . . . subject . . . bruce erickson . . . date . . . current . . . i had the opportunity to see bruce erickson in the office today . . . as you know . . . he is a fifty year old male who has had multiple lesions recently excised . . . with one in the medial thigh demonstrating a malignant fibrocystiocytoma . . . as you have previously discussed with him . . . wide excision and postoperative radiation treatment are considerations for him . . . (Paragraph) . . . today . . . options regarding reconstruction of the area were discussed with him . . . he is aware that our goal is to provide healthy tissue that would be able to tolerate the radiation treatment he would need as part of his particular treatment . . . in discussing this with him . . . options for local muscle transfer . . . including either sartorius or gracilis or even a portion of the adductors that may require a skin graft from the contralateral thigh in order to complete coverage . . . were mentioned . . . (Paragraph) . . . we feel this could give him the option of vascularized coverage within the area that would be irradiated . . . depending on the size of the defect . . . it may also be possible to use the sure close system in order to accomplish more direct closure . . . but our goal would be to accomplish whatever procedure would provide him with as good and early healing as possible in order to accomplish his radiation therapy . . . (Paragraph) . . . free tissue transfer was also discussed . . . and he is aware this might be an option if we felt the other local muscle flap options would be compromised due to the resectional surgery . . . he understands this . . . and we discussed additional risks and complications . . . scheduling is pending jointly through our offices . . . (Paragraph) . . . i appreciate the opportunity to participate in his care . . .

Is That a Fact?!

Treating some fractures with low-intensity sound waves cuts bone healing time by as much as 45 percent. The ultrasound device is similar in principle to the diagnostic ultrasound used to view the fetus during pregnancy. However, instead of sending and receiving sound waves to produce an image, the fracture-healing ultrasound sends sound waves in only one direction, so that they are absorbed into the bone.

JOB 75: Patient Data File

Dr. Patterson removed a crusted lesion from the back of his patient, Peter H. Walen, in the office today. Create a patient data file for Mr. Walen using the following information in Dr. Patterson's note of the procedure. Peter's date of birth is 8/15/64.

> Patient returns today. He has a crusted lesion in his back, which is removed using 1% Xylocaine with Epinephrine loc. Wd is closed with 4.0 nylon sutures. He has been instructed to have the stitches removed in approximately 10 days. To be up and about as tolerated. Certainly the area can get wet in approximately 2 days. He will call if a question or problem arises. His wife is a nurse and I have told him that she could remove the stitches if she feels comfortable with this.

JOB 76: Pathology Report

Ms. Georgia Hart, director of the Clinic's laboratory department, asks for help in formatting the following laboratory report on its department letterhead. Ms. Glazer asks you to type the report.

NAME: Peter H. Walen
DOB: 8/15/65
SEX: M
PHYSICIAN: Bruce Patterson, M.D.
SPECIMEN: Mid back skin lesion
DATE: (Current Date)
LAB. NO.: S-02265
GROSS: Received in formalin is a 2.7 x 1.0 cm tan-white skin segment excised to a depth of 0.8 cm. There is an eccentrically located, oblong, slightly raised lesion measuring 1.1 x 0.8 cm on the skin surface. Specimen is inked, serially sectioned, and entirely submitted excluding the tip as A and B.
MICROSCOPIC DIAGNOSIS: Skin and subcutaneum from mid back— inflamed seborrheic keratosis.

JOB 77: Patient Data File

Mr. Walen called the office today and talked with you about the lesion that was removed from his back. He indicated to you that his wife had taken the sutures out and that he was doing fine. Type a short note for his patient data file regarding his call.

Revise the pathology report (Job 76) if you have any errors in it. Resave it as *port*7, and print one copy for your portfolio.

Oncology

FOCUS ON MEDICAL CAREERS

RADIOGRAPHER/ SONOGRAPHER

Radiographers and sonographers assist physicians by obtaining images of internal organs, tissues, bones, and blood vessels to diagnose disease or injury.

Radiographers use x-rays to obtain images. Because radiation may be harmful, radiographers use protective equipment such as lead shields, follow rigid safety procedures, and wear film badges to monitor exposure. They determine how the x-rays will be taken, position patients correctly, adjust the equipment to give a clear view of the area to be x-rayed, and determine proper exposure settings.

Sonographers use ultrasound machines (which produce sound waves) to obtain images. The images are displayed on a monitor and can be videotaped or printed on film. Sonographers prepare patients by applying a sound-enhancing gel to the area to be viewed. Then they stroke the pad across the gel to create the image. Because sound waves are considered safe, sonography is often used when x-rays may be harmful.

Objectives

- Type documents from various kinds of copy: typed, handwritten, dictated.
- Format and revise one-page and multipage documents used in an oncology office: consultation reports, memos, operative reports, letters, announcements, pathology reports, labels, tables, and composed reports.
- Create letterhead and memo heading for unit.
- Extract pertinent information from a telephone call to prepare a written report.
- Prepare patient data files.
- Proofread documents; supply necessary capitalization and punctuation; and correct errors.

Terms to Know

adenocarcinoma	induration	nodes	premenopausal
carcinoma	medullary	occipital	remission
ecchymoses	monogram	palpable	subdigastric
hemoglobin	multifocal	polypectomy	

Today you will begin working in the Oncology Unit. Here you will be working with Dr. Lawrence Alexander, Director of the Oncology Unit; Dr. Mary Louise Amos; Dr. Lester Bodner; Ms. Carolyn Shetzer, R.N.; and Ms. Louise Roe, Administrative Assistant. Ms. Roe will be your supervisor.

Doctors of oncology specialize in the diagnosis and treatment of tumors in the body. Many of the patients in the unit have been referred by physicians in the surrounding area. Surgery is performed at Memorial Hospital. The Laboratory and Radiology Departments are used for testing.

Ms. Roe, your supervisor, will assist you with questions throughout your work in the Oncology Unit. The Procedures Manual will continue to serve as a good reference in addition to any special instructions provided with production jobs.

Document Processing

JOB 78: Unit Letterhead

Create the unit letterhead, and name it *oncolet*.

JOB 79: Patient Form Letter

The Accounting Department has asked each unit to send the following notice to their patients. Ms. Roe has edited the notice so that patients will know what department to call if they have questions concerning billing. Type the notice on letterhead, and leave 2 blank lines after *Notice to Patients*.

NOTICE TO PATIENTS:

If you received radiology, cardiology, respiratory therapy, EEG, or emergency services at Hayes Medical Clinic or Memorial Hospital, you may receive a separate bill from the clinic or the hospital. This bill will be based on the charges of the physician who interpreted the test results or the exam evaluation. Similarly, the hospital or clinic bill will include only the charges for the hospital or clinic services rendered, including care and supplies.

For questions concerning radiology charges, contact that office at Extension 7890. Please call our Accounting Office at Extension 7809 for information concerning other physicians' billing. For information regarding the hospital charges, please call the hospital billing office at 555-0177.

Thank you,

Hayes Medical Clinic

Memorial Hospital

Read through the entire report before typing.

Dr. Alexander assisted Dr. Patterson, director of the Surgery Unit, in the surgery of Elsie Buck. Ms. Buck had surgery as a result of a tightening of an artery to the left kidney as well as a renal cell cancer. The patient was admitted today, in room 1034, with history number 10065. Type the operative report on a Memorial Hospital Record form with a copy to Dr. Patrick Nehlson, director of the Urology Unit.

PREOP DIAGNOSIS: Acute left renal artery dissection following transluminal angioplasty for critical renal artery stenosis.

POSTOP DIAGNOSIS: Same.

OPERATION: Aorta-renal bypass.

ANESTHESIA: General—C. R. Cleveland, M.D.

INDICATIONS FOR SURGERY: The patient is a 77-year-old white female who was found to have a renal cell carcinoma involving her right kidney on recent CT scan of the abdomen done for staging of vulvar carcinoma. Subsequent arteriography showed a small left kidney measuring approximately 8 to 9 cm in length with a critical proximal renal artery stenosis that was non-osteo. The plan was to dilate the left renal artery lesion by transluminal angioplasty, and at a later date proceed with radical nephrectomy on the right side. If there was not sufficient recovery of renal function on the left side, partial nephrectomy was also considered. At the time of angioplasty today, there was satisfactory obliteration of the proximal stenosis, but the patient developed an intimal flap in the distal third of the renal artery at what was the termination of the angioplasty balloon. She was observed in the angiography suite and the dissection increased in severity, severely compromising flow in the renal artery. It appeared that the dissection was continuing into the hilum. She was, therefore, taken to the operating room in hopes of salvaging the kidney. She was given Mannitol preoperatively.

PROCEDURE: The patient was taken to the operating room and placed on the table in the supine position. A Foley catheter had previously been inserted into the bladder. A radial artery catheter was placed for blood pressure monitoring. After induction intubation, the patient was scrubbed and painted with Betadine from nipples to knees and draped in the usual sterile fashion. A Swan-Ganz catheter was floated by the right internal jugular approach for perioperative fluid management. The abdomen was entered through a left subcostal incision that was extended across the midline into the right side to the mid-clavicular line. Then, in the abdominal cavity, the small bowel was reflected toward the right side. The retroperitoneum over the aorta was opened and the renal vein identified and mobilized to the level of the ovarian vein, which was ligated and divided. The renal artery was exposed after reflecting the vein superiorly. It was distended with hemorrhage present in the adventitia consistent with dissection. To facilitate distal exposure, the left colon

(continued on next page)

was mobilized and reflected medially, allowing better exposure of the hilum. The dissection proceeded into the hilum to approximately 1.5 cm beyond the first major bifurcation. There was sub-adventitial hemorrhage extending well into the branch points. (*Paragraph*) The kidney was bluish in color except for the lower pole, which was pink through an accessory polar artery. Since it was not clear that there would be a patent vessel at the hilar level because of the extent of the dissection, the saphenous vein was not harvested and an inflow procedure was not performed first. The patient was given a second dose of Mannitol and 5,000 units of Heparin. After adequate circulation time, the proximal renal artery was controlled with a bulldog clamp, and a second bulldog clamp placed beyond the renal bifurcation. The renal artery was then divided approximately 1 cm proximal to the bifurcation. There was no thrombus noted in the true lumen. There was back-bleeding present from this. The thrombus was evacuated from the false lumen as best possible, and this area was gently irrigated with saline. The renal artery was then split longitudinally away from the area of dissection, which involved approximately 180° of the arterial circumference, mostly along the inferior side. The arteriotomy was on the superior side of the vessel at roughly the 9 o'clock position. Several tacking sutures of 6-0 Prolene suture were placed between the adventitia and true arterial lumen. A 6 mm stretched thin wall Gore-Tex graft was then brought into the operative field. It was cut obliquely and then sewn in an end-to-end fashion to the renal artery with care to include the elevated adventitia in the suture. The suture line was run with 6-0 Prolene suture. Following completion of this suture line, a 250 cc infusion of chilled Ringer's lactate containing Heparin, sodium bicarb, and Mannitol was infused. (*Paragraph*) The kidney blanched white except for the lower pole that had a separate blood supply. There was back-bleeding noted from the renal artery prior to the infusion. There was no leak apparent in the anastomosis. The graft was then passed under the colon and the infrarenal aorta exposed. The aorta was generally soft, but there was diffuse plaque evident on the arteriogram. The iliac vessels were ectatic and aneurysmal, and an iliac in-flow was not felt to be appropriate. The aortic clamps were placed. Arteriotomy was made and then the aortic punch used to enlarge the opening. There was some soft friable plaque present. This was carefully removed and vessel irrigated. The distal clamp was released from the aorta flush through the opening. The Gore-Tex graft was then trimmed and sewn in end-to-side fashion to the aorta with running 4-0 Prolene suture in parachute technique. The aorta was flushed with release of both clamps and the renal artery allowed to back-bleed prior to completion of the suture line. The distal clamp in the aorta was released first. The renal graft was compressed beyond its origin and the proximal aorta clamp then released. The proximal anastomosis was hemostatic. The renal graft was then opened. The renal artery distally appeared to extend

(continued on next page)

satisfactorily, and the kidney became pink. Several 6-0 Prolene sutures were required to provide complete hemostasis in the renal artery anastomosis as the toe of the anastomosis split slightly with restoration of in-flow pressure. (*Paragraph*) It should be noted that prior to clamping the aorta, the patient was given an additional 2,500 units of Heparin. Protamine sulfate was now given in a dose of 50 mg to reverse the total dose of 5,700 units given. The graft remained patent. Hemostasis was obtained throughout the operative field. The retroperitoneum was then closed with running 2-0 Vicryl. The spleen was inspected and found to be without injury. The colon was without injury as were the small bowel and duodenum. All packs were removed. Needle, sponge, and instrument counts were correct. The abdomen was then closed in layers with running 2-0 Vicryl for the peritoneum and posterior rectus sheath. The transversalis fascia and internal oblique fascia were similarly closed. The linea alba was approximated with interrupted 0 PDS suture. The anterior rectus sheath was approximated with running 0 PDS suture. The subcu was closed with 3-0 Vicryl; the skin, with staples. Betadine ointment and sterile dressings were applied. The feet were inspected and found to be well perfused with no evidence of a distal embolization. The patient was then rolled on her side and an epidural catheter placed. She tolerated the procedure without incident and was transferred to the recovery room following extubation. She was stable throughout the procedure. Prior to closure the right kidney was palpated and it was found to be freely mobile.

JOB 81: Announcement

An auxiliary is a support group for a hospital. It provides additional monies and personnel, e.g., operating a gift shop; wheelchair service; monies for magazines/books; aid to patients who need financial assistance.

Check with your instructor as to which graphics are available with your software, e.g., flags, balloons, a couple dancing, a chef, etc.

Hayes Medical Center's Auxiliary is sponsoring a dinner-dance to be held one month from Saturday. Ms. Roe asks that you help her publicize the event by creating an announcement from the copy that follows. Make the announcement appealing. Use different fonts, supply an appropriate graphic image, use the correct date, and use your name where indicated.

(Supply an appropriate graphic)
Hayes Medical Center Auxiliary
Annual Dinner Dance
Hilton Harbor View
Maumee, Ohio
(One month from Saturday)
7 p.m.
Tickets: $60 per person
Call (your name) or Louise Roe
at Extension 7884 today.

Is That a Fact?!

Exposure to light has extreme effects on body physiology, energy, sleep, and mood. For example, during the winter, less daylight can lead to depression, fatigue, and weight gain, sometimes referred to as seasonal affective disorder. Altering exposure to daylight also contributes to jet lag and causes disturbed sleep patterns in shift workers.

JOB 82: Unit Memo Heading

Create the unit memo heading, and name it **oncomemo**.

JOB 83: Handwritten Memo

Type the following memo, which informs all department heads and unit directors in the Center of the annual dinner dance. Include your name with Ms. Roe's in the heading, as you will be assisting her in making reservations.

To: All Department Heads and Unit Directors

From: Louise Roe and (your name)

Date:

Subject: Auxiliary's Annual Dinner Dance

The Auxiliary's Annual Dinner Dance will be held at the Hilton Harbor View in Maumee, on (one month from Saturday) at 7 p.m.

The Auxiliary is providing an enjoyable evening of food, fun, and music. The lavish dinner will feature prime rib of beef, broiled shrimp, baked crab cakes, and baked Alaska for dessert.

During dinner, John E. Kraeer III, one of the outstanding pianist-singers in the United States, will provide the entertainment. He plans to sing and play the oldies as well as any requests.

The GCees will provide the music for dancing. You may remember that The GCees captivated us at the annual dinner dance four years ago.

Tickets for the evening are $60 per person. More than half the cost of the dinner dance is being set aside by the Auxiliary to assist the Center in providing health care for the needy. Please encourage your employees to attend—the Auxiliary needs our help and we need their help.

Please post the enclosed announcements at appropriate places in your department or unit. Feel free to call either one of us if you have questions.

Enclosures: 10

JOB 84: Dictated Consultation Letter

Dr. Amos examined Deborah S. Powell in the office yesterday as a follow-up to radiation therapy. Type the consultation letter to Dr. Anthony Mercer, the referral physician, on Unit letterhead.

send this to doctor anthony mercer . . . four five six one north dixie highway . . . perrysburg . . . ohio . . . four three four five one . . . three five zero zero . . . dear tony . . . regarding . . . deborah s powell . . . date of birth . . . six . . . nine . . . forty nine . . . *(all caps)* . . . pathologic diagnosis . . . multifocal ductal carcinoma of the left breast with extensive intraductal carcinoma status post lumpectomy . . . re excision . . . axillary dissection . . . and radiation therapy . . . she just completed c m f chemotherapy . . . *(Paragraph)* . . . *(all caps)* . . . present status . . . she completed her chemotherapy nine days ago . . . she completed her radiation therapy two months ago . . . she is feeling well and has no complaints . . . her appetite and energy continue to improve . . . and she has noted no changes on her own self breast exam . . . *(Paragraph)* . . . she looks well . . . her neck is supple . . . there are no cervical . . . supraclavicular . . . infraclavicular . . . or axillary lymph nodes palpable . . . lungs are clear . . . heart is regular rate and rhythm . . . the left breast is smaller than the right . . . the surgical scar is deeply indented in the upper outer quadrant . . . there are no discrete palpable masses in either breast . . . the nipples are everted without discharge . . . her abdomen is soft and nontender . . . the liver and spleen are not enlarged . . . *(Paragraph)* . . . a left sided mammogram was obtained one week ago at memorial hospital . . . it appears satisfactory . . . we will await final radiologic interpretation . . . *(Paragraph)* . . . *(all caps)* . . . disposition . . . the patient is deemed in clinical remission . . . she is to return in six months with bilateral mammograms at that time . . .

JOB 85: Labels

There are a variety of commercially sold sizes and forms of labels that can be used for mailing as well as for folders/files. Check with your instructor to see if labels are available for this job.

Remember to type the last name first on file labels and to include courtesy titles on mailing labels.

Ms. Roe is creating files for new patients. Type the following patients' names on file-folder labels; then create mailing labels for these patients. You will find their addresses in the Patient Directory.

Elsie Mae Buck

Edgar Carnutte

Jane May Damer

Oscar Featherstone

Doris Goad

Jason Harris

Marcey Hughes

Jean McFadden

Deborah S. Powell

Leland K. Sawaia

Paul S. Wade

Is That a Fact?!

If your job calls for repetitive hand or finger work, take breaks every hour and exercise your hands and wrists to prevent carpal tunnel syndrome. A few warm-up exercises before starting to work and regular tension-relieving exercises throughout the workday can have a positive, preventive effect.

Dr. Bodner examined Paul S. Wade in the office today as a follow-up to his recent cancer surgery and radiation treatments. Type the letter to Dr. William Abbott, the primary physician.

send this to doctor william abbott . . . toledo medical center . . . four five two three monroe avenue . . . toledo . . . ohio . . . four three six zero five . . . two four zero zero . . . dear bill . . . regarding . . . paul . . . s . . . wade . . . date of birth . . . ten . . . three . . . forty eight . . . (all caps) . . . pathologic diagnosis . . . stage one a . . . (cap a) . . . cleaved b . . . (cap b) . . . cell follicular lymphoma in the left inguinal region . . . (all caps) . . . status . . . post surgical excision and radiation therapy . . . (all caps) . . . present status . . . mister wade completed his radiation therapy six weeks ago . . . he feels well and has no complaints . . . his appetite and energy are normal . . . he denies any . . . (cap b) . . . b symptoms . . . he looks well . . . his weight is down three pounds by intention . . . he now weighs one hundred seventy seven pounds . . . his neck is supple . . . there are no preauricular . . . postauricular . . . occipital . . . cervical . . . subdigastric . . . submental . . . supraclavicular . . . infraclavicular . . . axillary . . . abdominal . . . or inguinal lymph nodes to his scrotal sac exam . . . there is still that small three to four millimeter node in the right inguinal region that feels totally unchanged from his original examination . . . there is the surgical induration associated with the scar in the left . . . but this continues to resolve . . . his lungs are clear . . . heart is regular rate and rhythm . . . there is no bony tenderness . . . his abdomen is soft and nontender . . . the liver and spleen are not enlarged . . . there are no palpable masses . . . (Paragraph) . . . the patient has recovered well from his radiation therapy . . . he would like to pursue a second opinion and has requested that we make arrangements for him to be seen at the university of michigan hospital . . . we will make arrangements for that referral . . . we will also plan on seeing him back in three months with a c t . . . (all caps) . . . scan of the chest . . . abdomen . . . and pelvis . . . chest x ray . . . c b c . . . (all caps) . . . l d h . . . (all caps) . . . and s e d . . . (all caps) . . . rate . . .

A committee, formed by Ms. Roe and the nurses, is designing a health history questionnaire which patients will complete when they are first seen in the Unit. Type the portion of the questionnaire that has been completed on plain paper.

6. **Have you experienced any of the following problems <u>within the past six months</u>? CHECK YES OR NO FOR EACH CONDITION. If you check YES, please explain the condition.**

Condition	Yes	No	If Yes, Explain.
Loss of memory			
Blurred vision			
Difficulty hearing			
Difficulty swallowing			
Swollen neck			
Change in voice			
Shortness of breath			
Coughing up blood			
Pneumonia			
Cold (within past month)			
Chest pain			
Irregular heartbeat			
Artery or vein problem			
Leg pain when walking			
Swollen ankles			
Abdominal pain			
Nausea or vomiting			
Constipation			
Diarrhea			
Bloody stool			
Weight loss or gain			
Blood or pus in urine			
Incontinence			
More frequent urination			

Is That a Fact?!

Tendinitis is an inflammation in or around a tendon. Tendons are designed to withstand bending, stretching, and twisting, but they can become inflamed because of overuse, disease, or injuries. The pain can be significant, and continued use of the joint will make it worse. Tendinitis usually heals in about two weeks, but chronic tendinitis can take much longer if the tendons are not allowed to heal.

Jean D. McFadden returned to Dr. Bodner's office for a follow-up of surgery and radiation treatment of her right lung. Type this consultation letter, and send it to Dr. James Greene, her primary physician.

send this to doctor james a greene . . . four six seven main street . . . weston . . . ohio . . . four three five six nine . . . one zero zero one . . . dear doctor greene . . . regarding . . . jean . . . d . . . mcfadden . . . date of birth . . . ten . . . three . . . forty five . . . (*Paragraph*) . . . (*all caps*) . . . pathological diagnosis . . . right upper lobe non small cell carcinoma of the lung . . . stage roman numeral three b . . . (*cap b*) . . . (*all caps*) . . . present status . . . the patient continues on radiation therapy . . . she completes this course of treatment in two days . . . today we did a chest x ray . . . and there has not been much change in her mass . . . (*Paragraph*) . . . she is fairly comfortable on radiation therapy . . . and her pain is about the same . . . she is eating and maintaining her weight . . . (*Paragraph*) . . . her skin looks fine . . . her counts are satisfactory with a hemoglobin of twelve grams . . . (*Paragraph*) . . . in view of the present situation of her chest . . . i think we should give her a two week break in treatment . . . we will then have her back in two weeks for an assessment with a chest x ray . . . if the chest x ray shows improvement . . . we will then boost her residual mass . . . if the chest x ray shows no evidence of response . . . she will likely go to hospice . . . (*Paragraph*) . . . the patient is aware of the situation . . . i had a discussion today with her and her husband about the options . . . she and her husband wish to follow the above recommended process . . .

Georgia Hart, director of the Laboratory Unit, asked Ms. Roe for assistance in typing the following pathology report. Type the report for Ms. Hart on Laboratory Unit letterhead. The examination was 3 days ago.

NAME: Doris Goad
AGE: 40
SEX: F
PHYSICIAN: Mary Louise Amos, M.D.
DATE: (Current Date)
LAB. NO.: 300567
PRE- AND POST-OPERATIVE DIAGNOSES: Right breast mass; same.
SURGICAL PROCEDURE: Right breast biopsy.
TISSUE SPECIMENS: Right breast mass—fresh double suture at 12 o'clock, single suture at 9 'clock.

(continued on next page)

GROSS DESCRIPTION: The specimen labeled "right breast mass—fresh double suture at 12 o'clock, single suture at 9 o'clock" consists of 4 × 2.5 × 1.5 cm resection of fibroadipose tissue. It has a single suture and a double suture attached clinically designating as 9 and 12 o'clock, respectively. Cut surface discloses a centrally located tan-gray firm lesion with ill-defined margins that measure 1.8 × 1.7 × 0.8 cm. It involves all 4 quadrants of the specimen. The lesion extends up to one aspect of the resection margin.

Four quadrant, serial, clockwise sections of the entire specimen are submitted in cassettes labeled as A1, A2, B1, B2, C1, C2, D1, and D2. The tissue is procured for ER/PR receptor studies and DNA ploidy analysis.

JOB 90: Dictated Consultation Letter

Dr. Jean Harris referred her patient Marcey Hughes to the Oncology Unit for evaluation of a suspected cancerous left breast. Type Dr. Alexander's assessment.

send this to doctor jean harris . . . one two three two east michigan avenue . . . monroe . . . michigan . . . four eight one six one . . . two zero zero three . . . dear jean . . . regarding . . . marcey hughes . . . date of birth . . . twelve . . . eighteen . . . fifty eight . . . (*Paragraph*) . . . thank you for referring marcey hughes to us for evaluation . . . doctors amos and bodner assisted in this evaluation . . . (*Paragraph*) . . . (*all caps*) . . . pathological diagnosis . . . carcinoma of the left breast . . . intraductal comedo cancer . . . status post lumpectomy with negative margins . . . (*Paragraph*) . . . (*all caps*) . . . h p i . . . this is a forty one year old white female . . . premenopausal . . . with a strong history of breast cancer . . . who on routine mammography . . . was found to have abnormal calcifications in her left breast . . . the patient underwent a needle localization and excision by doctor amos on may nineteenth . . . nineteen ninety nine . . . a piece of tissue measuring five point three by three point four by two point one centimeters was removed . . . the biopsy showed no discrete nodules or masses . . . microscopically there was intraductal carcinoma . . . comedo type with a clean margin . . . the margins were close but clean . . . there was comment that seven of the twenty serial section fragments contained the comedo type of intraductal cancer . . . no invasive cancer was seen . . . (*Paragraph*) . . . the patient came to the unit to discuss management of her cancer . . . (*all caps*) . . . risk factors for breast cancer . . . the patient is forty one . . . she is premenopausal . . . she is a para two . . . gravida two . . . with the age of first delivery at thirty five . . . she has never taken hormones or birth control pills . . . a maternal aunt and a maternal grandmother both died of breast cancer and were postmenopausal . . . (*Paragraph*) . . . (*all caps*) . . . r o s . . . the patient has had problems since a devastating car accident at the age of eighteen . . . since

(continued on next page)

that time she has had memory problems and skeletal problems . . . she also has a history of sinus infections . . . hemorrhoid infections . . . and some stress urinary incontinence . . . she has frequent headaches . . . and she has had a history of colon polyps . . . *(Paragraph)* *(all caps)* . . . allergies . . . the patient is allergic to *(all caps and bold)* . . . demerol . . . codeine . . . and keflex . . . *(Paragraph)* *(all caps)* . . . medications . . . she is on no medication . . . *(all caps)* . . . p m h . . . her past surgeries include a polypectomy from the colon in nineteen ninety six . . . sinus surgery in nineteen eighty eight . . . a c section *(cap c)* in nineteen ninety three . . . a c section *(cap c)* in nineteen ninety-six . . . gallbladder and appendix removal in nineteen eighty seven . . . and repair of a torn liver in nineteen seventy six . . . *(Paragraph)* . . . *(all caps)* . . . social history . . . the patient is a nonsmoker . . . she lives with her spouse . . . she is a para two . . . gravida two s *(cap s)* . . . she has two children . . . ages six and two and a half . . . she is an activity therapist . . . but presently is at home with the children . . . her health care provider is doctor jean harris . . . *(Paragraph)* . . . *(all caps)* . . . family history . . . she has two maternal relatives with breast cancer . . . she has a strong family history of cancer with two aunts dying of colorectal cancer . . . one aunt dying of pancreatic cancer . . . a paternal grandmother dying of stomach cancer . . . and two paternal cousins dying of hodgkins disease . . . *(Paragraph)* . . . *(all caps)* . . . exam . . . *(all caps and indent 0.5 inch)* general . . . this is a young woman . . . forty one years old . . . who looks her stated age . . . vital signs . . . stable . . . lymphatics . . . there is no lymphadenopathy detected in the neck . . . cervical region . . . supraclavicular region . . . or infraclavicular regions . . . breasts . . . small with an elegant small healing scar in the upper outer quadrant of the left breast . . . some minimal ecchymoses and induration . . . there is a soft node in the left axilla measuring about one centimeter . . . probably related to the post excision biopsy . . . no other adenopathy is found . . . the right breast is satisfactory . . . except for fibrocystic changes . . . no evidence of disease is seen in the bones . . . the liver . . . or the lungs on clinical exam . . . extensive scarring that is all well healed . . . *(Paragraph)* . . . *(all caps)* . . . films . . . mammograms were reviewed with doctor bodner . . . microcalcification change in the present mammogram . . . d bin . . . *(cap d)* . . . device shows the microcalcifications have been removed . . . *(Paragraph)* . . . *(all caps)* . . . pathology . . . reviewed by doctor john p boland . . . shows a comedo intraductal carcinoma with clean margins . . . *(Paragraph)* . . . *(all caps)* . . . impression . . . carcinoma of the left breast . . . intraductal comedo carcinoma . . . status post lumpectomy . . . negative margins . . . stage zero . . . *(Paragraph)* . . . *(all caps)* . . . recommendation . . . the patient was seen by doctor alexander and doctor amos . . . her pathology was reviewed by doctor bodner . . . the patient was seen by the team and discussed at conference . . . the patient is an excellent candidate for breast preservation . . . and we discussed the options of therapy with her . . . it is the recommendation of the

(continued on next page)

group that this patient have no further surgery . . . we recommended a course of post-operative radiation therapy to the intact breast to save her breast . . . we also recommended no systemic therapy . . . we did not think she was eligible for any clinical studies . . . but we did recommend careful screening and physical exams on a regular basis because of her strong family history of cancer . . . *(Paragraph)* . . . the patient will discuss things further with doctor harris . . .

JOB 91: Composed Report

Mrs. Katherine Lyons called long distance and asked how Elsie Buck withstood her operation. She was indignant that she had not received any information about her condition. Mrs. Lyons indicated that she was a neighbor and that Ms. Buck had wanted her to know all facts.

You are aware that staff members may disclose patient information only to their immediate family members. You are unaware of any written agreement between Mrs. Lyons and Ms. Buck that would permit you to release any information.

Compose a one- or two-paragraph report, entitled *Patient Confidentiality*, relating what you would tell Mrs. Lyons. Refer to the Procedures Manual for the policy about patient confidentiality and the correct report format.

Is That a Fact?!

Using a cellular phone while driving quadruples the risk of having a collision. Having a "hands-free" phone appears to offer no advantage over a hand-held phone. People are more likely to have intense conversations that involve distracting problem solving while on the phone.

Dr. Bodner completed a follow-up examination of Jane Mae Damer's radiation therapy for cancer of the breast. Transcribe his report to Dr. Martin Thomas, the referral doctor.

send this to doctor martin thomas ... three four one five wildwood avenue ... jackson ... michigan ... four nine two zero four ... three two zero zero ... dear doctor thomas ... regarding ... jane mae damer ... date of birth ... october three ... nineteen fifty nine ... (*Paragraph*) ... (*all caps*) ... pathologic diagnosis ... stage one infiltrating tubular carcinoma of left breast ... (*Paragraph*) ... (*all caps*) ... status ... post lumpectomy and radiation therapy ... on tamoxifen ... (*cap t*) ... (*Paragraph*) ... (*all caps*) ... present status ... she completed her radiation two years and four months ago ... she lost her voice for two weeks and has seen doctor thomas ... who is treating her with medication ... she remains under stress with her older sister living with her ... her sister fell and broke her hip and ... therefore ... has been quite a challenge to manage ... miss damer has not noticed any changes on her own self breast exam ... (*Paragraph*) ... she looks well ... her weight is up three point five pounds in the last year to one hundred thirty five pounds ... her neck is supple ... there are no cervical ... supraclavicular ... infraclavicular ... or axillary lymph nodes palpable ... lungs are clear ... heart is regular rate and rhythm ... the breasts are symmetric with a good cosmetic outcome ... she has a scar on the upper aspect of each breast ... there are no palpable masses in either breast ... the nipples are everted without discharge ... her abdomen is soft and nontender ... her liver is not enlarged ... (*Paragraph*) ... a left sided mammogram was obtained on january sixteenth ... nineteen ninety nine ... and is satisfactory ... she received her bilateral mammograms at her visits with doctor thomas ... and by her report ... these have also been normal ... (*Paragraph*) ... (*all caps*) ... disposition ... the patient is deemed in clinical remission ... she is to see doctor thomas in six months with bilateral mammogram then ... she is to return here in one year with a left sided mammogram at that visit ...

Portfolio

Revise the pathology report if you have any errors in it. Resave the document as *port8*, and print one copy for your portfolio.

UNIT 9 Dermatology

FOCUS ON MEDICAL CAREERS

MEDICAL TRANSCRIPTIONIST

*M*edical transcriptionists create health records by transcribing physicians' dictation or notes. Typically, this information includes the diagnoses and treatments of patients. Transcriptionists may work for a single physician or for many physicians.

Excellent typing skills and a good command of medical terminology are essential to ensure that medical terms are used accurately and spelled correctly. Transcriptionists often need to edit physicians' notes to be sure that grammar and usage are correct and to create an understandable and easy-to-follow medical record.

Medical transcriptionists may work in the hospital or other clinical setting, a physician's office, an insurance company, for a medical transcribing firm, or out of their homes.

Objectives

- Type documents from various kinds of copy: typed, rough draft, handwritten, dictated.
- Format and revise one-page and multipage documents used in a dermatology office: consultation report, patient data file, memo, patient rights and responsibilities, table.
- Create letterhead and memo heading for unit.
- Extract pertinent information from consultation reports to prepare patient data files.
- Proofread documents; supply necessary capitalization and punctuation; and correct errors.

Terms to Know

antecubital	hyperkeratotic	molluscum	recalcitrant
axilla	inguinal	neurodermatitis	sebopsoriasis
cheilitis	keratoacanthoma	pedunculated	seborrheic dermatitis
eczematous	lichen urticatus	pustular bullae	telangiectatic
erythema	lichenification	pustules	varicella
excoriations			

Today you will begin working in the Dermatology Unit. You will be assisting Dr. Clayton Lee Longtree, Director; Dr. Susan Meiske-Rose; and Ms. Justine Harris, office assistant. Your supervisor will be Ms. Harris.

The physicians and specialists in the Dermatology Unit specialize in the diagnosis and treatment of skin disorders. Testing is conducted in the Laboratory and Radiology Departments as well as in the unit's own rooms. Minor outpatient surgery is performed within the unit.

Document Processing

JOB 93: Dermatology Unit Letterhead

Create the Dermatology Unit letterhead, and name it *dermlet*.

JOB 94: Consultation Letter

Refer to the Procedures Manual for the correct format of a consultation letter.

Dr. Longtree examined Henry Bolden in the office yesterday for a facial rash. Type the consultation letter to Dr. Anthony Mercer, the referring physician.

> Anthony Mercer, M.D., 4561 North Dixie Highway, Perrysburg, Ohio 43451-3500; the patient's date of birth is 10/11/63.
>
> I examined Henry Bolden on (*use yesterday's date*). He was complaining of a facial rash.
>
> Examination of this patient revealed sebopsoriasis and extensive seborrheic dermatitis over his upper eyebrows, nasolabial fold, and extending to the subnasal region.
>
> A prescription of SS (Medid) shampoo was given the patient to be applied every other day. The patient was also given a prescription of menthol, LCD, salicylsalicylic acid in Valisone lotion to be applied to the face 2× daily for 2 weeks and then 1× daily. In addition, the patient was given a prescription of menthol, LCD, salicylsalicylic acid in Lidex Ointment to be applied topically 2× a day for 2 weeks, then 1× a day at h.s.
>
> I will see this patient again in 2 weeks and keep you updated on the progress.

JOB 95: Patient Data File

The patient data file should contain only information pertinent to the patient's care. When extracting information from a consultation report to create the file, do not include information such as (1) the statement that the physician will keep the referring physician updated and (2) the closing lines.

Important portions of consultation reports may be used to create patient data files. Retrieve the sections indicated below from the report in Job 94 to create this file for Henry Bolden.

(*Yesterday's Date*)

Chief Complaint:	**Facial rash.**
Consultation:	(*Paragraph 2*)

(*Paragraph 3*)

I will see this patient again in 2 weeks.

JOB 96: Consultation Letter

Use the current date.

Type symbols in medical documents whenever possible, e.g., 4 × a day.

Dr. Luther Adler referred his patient, Otto Kauffman, to Dr. Meiske-Rose. Mr. Kauffman has had a rash for the past six to eight months. Type this report of the examination.

Luther Adler, M.D., Monroe Clinic, 4523 Monroe Avenue, Toledo, Ohio 43605-2400; the patient's birth date is 4/26/63.

I examined Otto Kauffman on (*last Friday's date*) with a chief complaint of rash, on and off, for the past 6 to 8 months.

The patient has cats and dogs in the house. He stated that he has to sleep on a night chair, at which time he itches a lot while in the chair. The patient has had the house fumigated 2 × for fleas that were noted on the cats and dogs.

Examination of this patient revealed mild erythema and excoriations with lichenified skin extending over the arms and legs and a few pustular lesions noted over the hands. The pretibial region of the legs revealed some asteatotic eczema. Assessment was that of a mite (flea bite ruled out) with lichen urticatus and neurodermatitis component.

The patient was treated with Elimite; he also was advised to repeat this treatment if he was still pruritic at the end of 4 days. The patient also was given a prescription of menthol, precipitated sulfur, triamcinolone, and Dermasil lotion to be applied 3 × daily to the area over the chest and arms.

The asteatotic eczema on the legs was treated with menthol, triamcinolone, and Dermasil, to be applied 4 × a day for 2 weeks, then 3 × a day for 2 weeks, and then 1 × a day for 2 weeks. The patient was given an injection of Depo-Medrol and advised to compress this area 3 × a day for 15 minutes.

I will keep you informed on his progress.

JOB 97: Patient Data File

Use the consultation letter date.

Format a patient data file for Mr. Kauffman using the necessary information from Dr. Luther Adler's consultation letter in Job 96.

JOB 98: Dermatology Unit Memo Heading

Create the unit memo heading, and name it **dermmemo.**

JOB 99: Memo

Set off a name used in direct address with commas, e.g., *You were outstanding, Al, with* . . .

Proofread your finished document. Format the title of the television program in italic.

Dr. Longtree wrote the following memo to Dr. Alvin K. Larson of the Plastic Surgery Unit following Dr. Larson's appearance on television last Sunday. Type the memo. Use *Television Appearance* as the subject line.

Dr. Larson (please use his complete name and title), What a surprise I had Sunday when I tuned in my television to Medical Breakthroughs. You were outstanding, Al, with your discussion of plastic surgery and its possible psychological implications. Your discussion was to the point with current research and medical practice. I can understand why physicians in your field of medicine look to you for guidance. I hope that all of our colleagues were able to see the program.

I was also pleased to learn of your recent recognition by the local NAACP for medical assistance in the greater Toledo metropolitan area. Again congratulations on both jobs well done.

Copy to Dr. S. Novak

Is That a Fact?!

People with pacemakers can safely use cellular phones as long as they don't carry the phones in a shirt or jacket pocket over their chests. Placing cellular phones close to the chest can disrupt a pacemaker's natural rhythm. Holding the phone against the ear does not appear to have the same risk.

Dr. Longtree asked you to type a final copy of the following rough-draft document single-spaced. It informs patients about their rights and responsibilities while they are in the outpatient clinic or hospital. Number the second page at the bottom center.

Each has the to

<u>Patient Rights</u> AND RESPONSIBILITIES

~~Patient rights~~ ~~Include the Right:~~) No Bold

1. To be treated with consideration, respect, and full acceptance of the patient's dignity and individuality, including privacy in treatment and care for personal needs.

2. To be free of medical, psychological, physical, and chemical (neglect) or (abuse).

3. To be free from physical constraint, with *the* exception of an emergency where a restraint is necessary *to* protect the patient *or others,* from injury ~~to himself or others,~~ and is authorized by the attending doctor.

4. To refuse treatment, withdraw consent for treatment or ~~to~~ give *contingent* consent for treatment.

5. To have medical and financial ~~data~~ *records* ~~kept~~ *confidential,* ~~in trust and~~ the release of ~~such records~~ *which* shall be by written consent of the patient or the patient's surrog*ate* ~~surrogot~~ except as other wise required or permitted by law.

6. To *Have* ac*c*ess to the patients medical record.

7. To be advised of rates and charges prior to admission ~~(for services)~~ or prior *be advised* to change *s* in rates, *and* charges or services, and informed of possible ~~three-~~ ~~two~~ party coverage *for services.*

8. To be advised on the *Hayes Medical* center's policy regarding *honoring wills* living ~~trusts~~.

9. To be included in decisions regarding care and treatment.

10. To associate and communicate privately with persons of the patient's choice.

11. To have access to a telephone.

12. To submit grievances without retaliation.

13. To be informed of the proposed surgical procedures and ~~the~~ risks.

14. To exercise other civil rights and religious beliefs.

(continued on next page)

Each Patient ~~Responsibilities Include:~~ (is le for) no bold

1. Providing, ~~to the best of his knowledge,~~ accurate and complete information.

2. Reporting unexpected changes in his/her condition and ~~whether he clearly~~ understanding a PLANNED course of action and what is expected ~~of him/her,~~ / care physician.

3. Following the treatment plan proposed by the ~~doctor~~ primarily ~~responsible for his/her care;~~

4. Keeping appointments, ~~or if unable to~~ notifying the appropriate person; if unable to keep an appointment, or

5. Being responsible for his/her own actions if ~~he/she~~ refuses treatment or ~~does~~ not following directions.

6. Assuming that ~~the financial duties of his/her~~ obligations health care are fulfilled as soon as possible.

7. Following the Hayes Medical Center's rules and regulations affecting patient care and conduct,

8. Being considerate of the rights of other patients and Center personnel and assisting in the control of noise and the number of visitors, ~~and~~

9. Being respectful of ~~the~~ property of persons belonging to other ~~and of the~~ Center's. or to Hayes Medical

JOB 101: Composed Memo

Dr. Longtree asks that you write a memo to Dr. Steven Novak, Chief Administrator, informing him that the Committee on Patient Rights and Responsibilities has met and completed the first draft of the form. Ask him to review the draft copy you are enclosing, mark any suggestions, and then return the document to Dr. Longtree within one week.

UNIT 9: DERMATOLOGY   117

JOB 102: Dictated Consultation Letter

Proofread your finished document.

Dr. Blake K. Lyons referred her patient, Lisa Q. Davis, to Dr. Meiske-Rose for consultation. Transcribe the report of the examination and prescribed treatment of Ms. Davis's rash.

this letter goes to doctor blake k lyons . . . eight six seven hubbell street . . . maumee . . . ohio . . . four three five three seven . . . one zero zero two . . . dear doctor lyons . . . regarding lisa q davis . . . date of birth . . . two . . . twelve . . . seventy eight . . . i examined lisa q davis today with the chief complaint of rash over the shoulder and digits . . . *(Paragraph)* . . . examination of this area revealed erythmea and pustular bullae noted over the right shoulder . . . as well as some hemorrhagic changes and some bullae noted over the digits . . . it is my feeling that this is an irritant allergic contact dermatitis possibly due to the neosporin *(capital n)* that was applied to this area status post rash . . . *(Paragraph)* . . . the patient was treated with depo medrol *(capital d, hyphen before the capital m)* . . . and was given sixty milligrams im *(capitals)* . . . in addition . . . a prescription was written for phenol and calamine to be applied three times daily . . . and she was started on prednisone . . . twenty milligrams . . . to be reduced over a fifteen day period . . . *(Paragraph)* . . . i will see this patient again in three days in the office and keep you updated on her progress . . . *(Paragraph)* . . . thank you for this referral . . .

Is That a Fact?!

Some athletes believe that using smokeless tobacco helps them to relax, concentrate, and stay alert, and so improve their performance on the field. Contrary to what big-league baseball players believe, they don't gain any benefit in batting, fielding, or pitching over players who abstain. However, they do raise their risk of developing oral cancer, tooth damage, and gum disease. In one study of baseball players, almost half of the tobacco users had potentially precancerous oral lesions, and one-third had serious, permanent gum recession.

JOB 103: Patient Data File

Create a patient data file for Lisa Davis, extracting data from Dr. Meiske-Rose's consultation report.

JOB 104: Memo

Read through the entire memo before typing.

Do not capitalize words such as *lower, upper,* and *greater* except when they are part of a geographic name that is well established, whether actual or imaginative, e.g., *Upper Montclair, greater Toledo area.*

Mr. Leland Smith, Director of Personnel, has been named the Center's chairperson for the annual United Fund Drive. He has asked you to assist him in this year's campaign. Type the following handwritten memo to all departments and units; provide an appropriate subject line.

We have been asked again to help the United Fund Drive for the greater Toledo area. Hayes Medical Center has always been a leader in assisting the drive. In addition, it has always had a representative on the local board of directors. This year I am pleased to represent the Center.

I am sure many of you have met (your full name), who is currently employed in the Dermatology Unit. I have asked (your personal title and last name) to assist me with the general drive and our own drive at the Center.

Attached is a table showing department and unit representatives, goals, and the proposed total for the Center. Your representative will inform you how you may contribute to this year's campaign. We will update the table weekly with the monies collected to date and will circulate it to all employees.

Thank you for your help in making this a successful drive.

Is That a Fact?!

Warts are caused by the human papilloma virus, which enters the skin through a cut or scratch. There are many folk remedies for warts, but one that may have some validity is rubbing the wart with a slice of raw potato or the inner side of a banana skin. Both of these contain chemicals that may dissolve the wart.

Read through the table before typing.

Format the following table on plain paper. Add *Hayes Medical Center* as the title and *United Fund Drive* as the subtitle. Center it horizontally and vertically. Total the third column. This table is the enclosure for Job 104.

Department/Unit	Representative	Goal ($)	Collected to Date
Accounting	S. Rose	1,500	
Administration	L. Baynes	1,500	
Admissions	L. Moffett	500	
Allergy/Immunology	M. Tyson	2,000	
Cardiovascular	C. Thomas	2,000	
Dermatology	J. Harris	2,000	
Head and Neck	D. Oaster	2,000	
Internal Medicine	J. Wallace	2,000	
Laboratory	X. Zhu	1,000	
Medical Records	D. Benegela	500	
Oncology	L. Roe	2,000	
Personnel	L. Smith	500	
Pharmacy	S. Lado	500	
Plastic Surgery	L. Albert	2,000	
Surgery	J. Glazer	2,000	
Radiology	J. Boland	500	
Urology	L. Albertson	2,000	
TOTAL			

JOB 106: Consultation Letter

Dr. Jean Harris referred her patient, Thomas E. Mercer, for consultation with Dr. Longtree. Type Dr. Longtree's report of the examination and prescribed treatment for Mr. Mercer's redness in the facial skin.

Jean Harris, M.D.; 1322 East Michigan Avenue; Monroe, MI 48161-2003. The patient's birth date is November 23, 1968.

Thomas E. Mercer visited the office on (*yesterday's date*) with the chief complaint of redness in his facial skin.

Examination revealed facial erythema over the scalp and chest, extending into the axillary region also. It is my feeling that this is seborrheic dermatitis.

The patient was treated with precipitated sulfur and Elocon lotion to be applied 2 × daily. I advised Nizoral to his scalp at least 3 × weekly. We will wean the patient to 1 application of the Elocon cream to the face if the current treatment prescribed warrants good results.

I will keep you updated on the progress.

JOB 107: Patient Data File

Create a patient data file for Thomas Mercer.

Portfolio

Choose one of the consultation letters to revise if you have any errors in it. Resave the document as *port9*, and print one copy for your portfolio.

Is That a Fact?!

Do you reach for the eyedrops when your eyes are red and irritated? If so, you may want to know that some non-prescription drops can give you a case of pinkeye, the common name for conjunctivitis. Conjunctivitis is an inflammation of the eyelid lining and white of the eye. It's usually caused by allergies, a virus, or a bacterial infection. Although it is uncomfortable, it is usually a harmless condition that makes eyes red, itchy, and gritty-feeling.

Internal Medicine

FOCUS ON MEDICAL CAREERS

PHYSICIANS' ASSISTANT

Physician's assistants provide direct patient care under the supervision and instruction of a licensed physician. Assistants' duties include taking a patient's medical history, performing physical examinations, and performing diagnostic and therapeutic procedures. In addition, assistants can also write prescriptions.

Physicians' assistants work in a variety of settings including physicians' private practices, hospitals, clinics, nursing homes, and government or community agencies. They may also work with medical assistants or teach in physicians' assistant programs once they have had appropriate clinical experience.

Objectives

- Type documents from various kinds of copy: typed, rough draft, handwritten, dictated.
- Format one-page and multipage documents used in an internal medicine office: patient data file, letters, physical examination report, consultations report, AIDS information sheet.
- Create letterhead for unit.
- Prepare patient data files from telephone calls for prescriptions.
- Compose a short report.
- Proofread documents; supply necessary capitalization and punctuation; and correct errors.

Terms to Know

apraxia	dorsal	hemoptysis	organomegaly
ascites	dorsum	hydronephrosis	osteopath
aspirated	dysfunction	leukocytes	pedis
ataxia	dysphagia	lithiasis	prothrombin
cerebellar	dysuria	micturition	scoliosis
cerebellum	extraocular	morphology	spondylosis
demyelination	granulomatous	myelogram	ulcerate
dextrorotation	hematuria		

Today you will begin work in the Internal Medicine Unit. You will work with Dr. Nancy Veenstra, director of Internal Medicine; Dr. Daniel Barnett; Dr. James Emerson; Dr. Michael McGinty; Ms. Nancy Ann Stevens, R.N.; and Ms. Jackie Wallace, office assistant. Ms. Wallace will be your supervisor.

Although Dr. McGinty is associated with the Center, his primary office is in Toledo.

Doctors of internal medicine specialize in the diagnosis and treatment of the internal structures of the body. Minor surgery is performed in the unit examination rooms.

Document Processing

JOB 108: Internal Medicine Unit Letterhead

Create the unit letterhead, and name it *interlet*.

JOB 109: Dictated Letter

Medical personnel often must provide information to insurance and legal firms about patients' injuries that result from accidents.

Use the abbreviated title *Esq.* for *Esquire* with a name in an address (e.g., *Robert Levin, Esq.*). Omit a personal title such as *Mr.* in the address.

Read through the entire letter before you type it.

Insert a hyphen after a prefix ending in *i* or *a* if the base word also begins with the same letter, e.g., *anti-inflammatories*.

Dr. Veenstra's patient, Tony Anthony, was injured in an automobile accident in February of last year. The case has been pending for some time, and Mr. Anthony's attorney requires further medical information before the insurance settlement can be rendered to the involved parties. Transcribe the letter for Dr. Veenstra.

> this letter goes to . . . robert levin . . . esquire . . . abbott . . . levin . . . and bohlstaadt (that's b o h l s t a a d t) . . . sixty seven shrock road . . . toledo . . . ohio . . . four three six zero five . . . one zero zero four . . . dear mister levin . . . regarding tony anthony . . . date of birth . . . tony anthony was involved in an automobile accident on february first of last year . . . he stated that he was a passenger and was asleep at the time of the accident . . . he further stated that he did not know what happened to cause the accident or what happened during the accident . . . he denied hitting his head or losing consciousness . . . following the accident . . . mister anthony went to the memorial hospital emergency room . . . x rays taken at the hospital were negative . . . (*Paragraph*) . . . mister anthony was examined in our office on february thirteenth . . . (*last year*) . . . with complaint of pain in the upper back and shoulders as well as headaches . . . a physical examination revealed increased muscle spasm in the right middorsal and upper dorsal areas and left cervical area . . . heel and toe walking was within normal limits . . . diagnoses include dorsal and cervical somatic dysfunction . . . treatment consisted of osteopathic manipulative therapy . . . hydroc packs . . . and anti inflammatories . . . (*Paragraph*) . . . he returned to the office on februrary nineteeth . . . (*last year*) . . . with complaint of pain in the upper back

(continued on next page)

and neck . . . i noted increased muscle spasm in his right middorsal and upper dorsal areas . . . in addition . . . he felt pain with flexion and left rotation . . . treatment consisted of an anti inflammatory . . . and the patient was advised to return for hydroc packs two times a week for two weeks . . . *(Paragraph)* . . . mister anthony was seen again on february twenty first . . . *(last year)* . . . with the complaint of increased pain in his neck . . . the treatment consisted of hydroc packs . . . and he was referred to an orthopedist . . . *(Paragraph)* . . . i last examined mister anthony on march sixth . . . *(repeat last year again)* . . . i noted a slight decreased left rotation and increased muscle spasm in his middorsal area as well as decreased side bending bilaterally . . . treatment consisted of hydroc packs . . . an anti-inflammatory . . . and osteopathic manipulative therapy . . . *(Paragraph)* . . . if i may be of further assistance . . . please let me know . . .

JOB 110: Physical Examination Report

Physicians may record the results of a physical examination with handwritten notes, by audiotape, or dictate to a transcriber or a computer. Some practices use a printed form on which the physician records the applicable information.

Hyphenate compound adverbs appearing after a verb, e.g., employed full-time.

Read through the handwritten notes prior to typing the report.

Dr. Barnett recorded the following notes of a physical examination that he performed on Evan Demoulin today. Mr. Demoulin was experiencing rectal bleeding and hematuria (blood or red blood cells in the urine). His date of birth is 5/10/60.

On unit letterhead type the title *PHYSICAL EXAMINATION REPORT* in bold and underlined 2 lines below the unit name. Then space down 2 lines to begin the body. Type headings in all caps and bold and indent subheadings 0.5 inch from the left margin and type them in caps and lowercase.

Translate Dr. Barnett's brief notes into complete sentences where possible.

PHYSICAL EXAMINATION REPORT

NAME: *Evan Demoulin*

DATE OF EXAM:

CHIEF COMPLAINT: *Rectal bleeding and hematur\ia.*

HISTORY OF PRESENT ILLNESS: *2 mos ago following micturition, patient passed 1 tsp of dark red blood per urethra. Before that he had noted some red staining of his underwear.*

No associated dysuria, hematuria, or frequency.

Approx. 1 mo ago patient developed rectal bleeding; was described as intermittent & associated with pruitus ani. Bright red blood has been passed since that time intermittently, not associated w/stooling. No pain with defecation; having up to 5 BMs/day & describes tenesmus.

No history of significant weight loss, anorexia, dysphagia, vomiting, anal injury was noted.

(continued on next page)

PRESENT MEDICATIONS: *None*

ALLERGIES: *No known drug allergies. Has been treated in the past for exposure to tuberculosis, but not for tuberculosis itself.*

PAST MEDICAL HISTORY:

Surgeries: *No prior surgeries.*

Accidents and Injuries: *Motor vehicle accident, 1995; there was loss of consciousness and some neck strain w/o vertebral injury.*

FAMILY HISTORY: *3 sisters and 2 brothers, all reportedly alive and well. No family history of bowel cancer known.*

SOCIAL HISTORY: *Engaged. Employed full time. Smokes approx. 1 pk. of cigs/day; drinks nearly 2 qts. beer daily. Has no history of use of illicit drugs.*

REVIEW OF SYSTEMS:

General: *Has lost some weight in recent months; admits this is due to conscious attempt to reduce weight. No fever or night sweats.*

Skin: *No rash or moles.*

Head: *Reports headaches; not discussed on this visit.*

Eyes: *Has a cataract in the left eye. Reports eye pain.*

Nose: *No polyps or nasal discharge.*

Cardiorespiratory: *No cough, sputum, hemoptysis, chest pain, dyspnea, wheezing. No history of rheumatic fever or hypertension.*

GI: *As described above. Stools are described as dry and hard. No history of jaundice.*

GU: *As described above. No prior history of renal calculi. No history of penile discharge, prostatitis.*

Musculoskeletal: *Positive for back pain.*

Metabolic: *No history of diabetes, thyroid dysfunction, or hyperlipidemia.*

Hematologic: *No history of anemia or lymphadenopathy.*

PHYSICAL EXAMINATION:

Vital Signs: *Ht 5'7", wgt 170 lb., pulse 60/minute and regular, respirations 16/minute, BP w/large cuff 88/54.*

General: *Alert, well built, well nourished, in no apparent distress.*

Hands: *No clubbing.*

(continued on next page)

HEENT: *Pupils equal and reactive to light. Ophthalmoscopy revealed a cataract in the left eye. The right fundus is w/in normal limits w/sharp disk margins. No hemorrhages or exudates. Sclerae nonicteric. Tympanic membranes pearly grey bilaterally.*

Neck: *Supple.*

Chest: *Clear to auscultation with good air entry bilaterally.*

Abdomen: *The abdomen is soft, nontender with no masses, no organomegaly and no ascites.*

Rectal: *Negative for mass. Normal sphincter tone. Stool hemocult not performed.*

Genitalia: *No testicular masses or penile or groin lesions.*

Extremities: *Dorsalis pedis pulses are +2 and equal. No ankle edema.*

Neurologic: *Cranial nerves 2-12 are grossly intact. Tone w/in normal limits. Power 5/5 in all 4 extremities. Coordination by finger-to-nose finger test is within normal limits. Deep tendon reflexes are +2 and symmetrical. Sensation grossly intact.*

PHYSICIAN: *D. Barnett*

Is That a Fact?!

Although its focus is on food, anorexia nervosa is an illness of the mind. Often it begins with a desire to lose a few pounds. It then becomes compulsive behavior. Food intake is minimized until eating is almost eliminated. The result of this self-starvation and major weight loss can cause hormonal disturbances, anemia, irregular heartbeat, brittle bones, and other problems. If left untreated, it can cause death.

Dr. Daniel Barnett referred his patient, Gail Ehret, to Dr. McGinty for consultation. Dr. McGinty's office is in Toledo, but he often sees patients at the Center. Any of his correspondence, therefore, is done on Toledo office letterhead. Ms. Wallace typed and edited the following report of Ms. Ehret's visit to send to Dr. Barnett. Use Dr. McGinty's Toledo letterhead for this document. The letterhead is stored on your data disk as *toledo.*

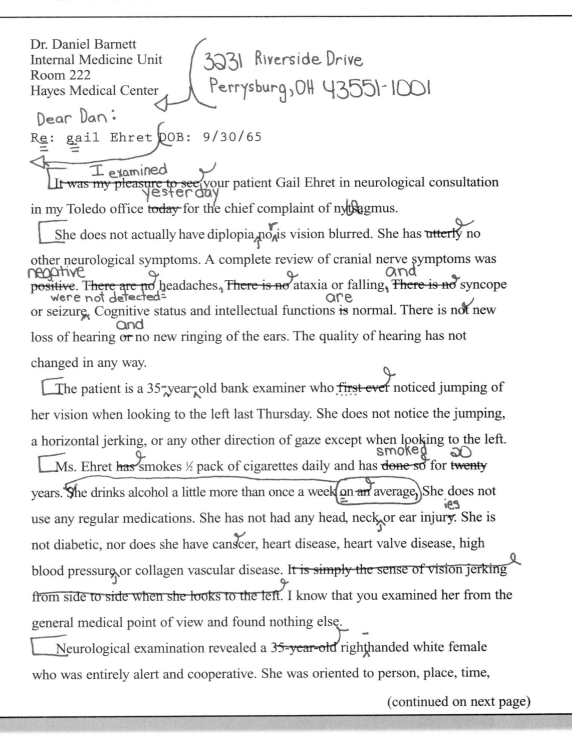

Dr. Daniel Barnett
Internal Medicine Unit
Room 222
Hayes Medical Center

3231 Riverside Drive
Perrysburg, OH 43551-1001

Dear Dan:

Re: gail Ehret DOB: 9/30/65

I examined
It was my pleasure to see your patient Gail Ehret in neurological consultation
yesterday
in my Toledo office today for the chief complaint of nystagmus.

She does not actually have diplopia, no is vision blurred. She has utterly no

other neurological symptoms. A complete review of cranial nerve symptoms was
negative
positive. There are no headaches, There is no ataxia or falling, and There is no syncope
were not detected=
are
or seizure. Cognitive status and intellectual functions is normal. There is not new
and
loss of hearing or no new ringing of the ears. The quality of hearing has not

changed in any way.

The patient is a 35-year-old bank examiner who first ever noticed jumping of

her vision when looking to the left last Thursday. She does not notice the jumping,

a horizontal jerking, or any other direction of gaze except when looking to the left.
smoked   20
Ms. Ehret has smokes ½ pack of cigarettes daily and has done so for twenty

years. She drinks alcohol a little more than once a week on an average, She does not
ies
use any regular medications. She has not had any head, neck, or ear injury. She is

not diabetic, nor does she have cancer, heart disease, heart valve disease, high

blood pressure, or collagen vascular disease. It is simply the sense of vision jerking

from side to side when she looks to the left. I know that you examined her from the

general medical point of view and found nothing else.

Neurological examination revealed a 35-year-old righthanded white female

who was entirely alert and cooperative. She was oriented to person, place, time,

(continued on next page)

and situation with normal speech, affect, and mood. There was no sign of aphasia or other language disorder, agnosia, or apraxia. Remote, recent, and retentive memories were intact. Blood pressure was 78/110/78, pulse 64 and regular, weight 139 lb, height 5'6".

Examination of cranial nerves II-XII showed a normal sense of smell bilaterally. Visual fields were full to gross confrontation. Ophthalmoscopy was normal bilaterally. Discs were flat. There was no sign of hemorrhage or exudate. Vasculature was normal. Pupilary function was normal bilaterally. Pupils were 4 mm and appropriately reactive to light and accommodation. Extraocular movements were normal except for horizontal nystagmus on right lateral gaze. This is also partially evident on upward gaze in the midline and very slightly evident on downward gaze, but there does not seem to be nystagmus on right lateral gaze. Opticokinetic nystagmus was normal. Muscles of mastication and facial expression were normal. Facial sensation was normal. Corneal reflexes were normal bilaterally. Weber's sign and rinne's sign were normal. The palate moved well. Gag reflex was normal bilaterally. Sternocleidomastoid and trapezius muscles were normal bilaterally. The tongue was in the mid-line and normally formed. Tympanic membranes were normal bilaterally.

Motor examination revealed normal bulk, tone, strength, and movement of all muscle groups of the neck, torso, and the upper and lower limbs. Casual gait examination was normal. Posture and stance were normal. In tandem gait was normal. Reflexes were all 1-1/2+ and bilaterally symmetrical. Toe signs were bilaterally flexor. There were no grasp or frontal lobe release reflexes.

Romberg's signs was absent. Sensory examination revealed normal pain and temperature, position, vibratory, and touch sense everywhere. Stereognosis was normal. Corticosensory testing was normal.

Cerebellar examination revealed normal finger to nose, heel to shin, and rapid alternating movements bilaterally. There was no tremor.

Examination of the spine was normal. Spurlings sign was negative. Carotids were 1-1/2+ bilaterally without bruit or thrill over the carotids, superclavicular fossae, eyes, or any part of the cranium. Skin showed no evidence of neurocutaneous

(continued on next page)

disease. The ears were normal externally. Tmj examination was normal bilaterally.

IMPRESSION: I can find no reason for the nystagmus at the present time. Peripheral disorders such as Meniere's disease, primarily vestibular or inner ear, must be considered, but there has been no vertigo and no hearing loss or tinnitus. We will check these peripheral possibilities with an ENG, an audiogram and a brain stem auditory evoked response procedures.

Of course, more worrisome is a tumor such as acoustic neuroma or cerebellar tumor. There were no segmental brain stem signs to confirm this. Finally, we will ask for blood work to rule out collagen vascular disease, although this seems unlikely. Nonetheless, a brain MRI scan including internal auditory canals is in order.

We will keep in close contact with Ms. Ehret and try to have the tests performed as quickly as possible, especially a brain MRI scan, but I can find no other objective neurological abnormality at all. Naturally, the MRI scan will also help rule out demyelinating disease as a consideration.

Thank you for referring this patient. I appreciate the opportunity to participate in her neurological care.

Sincerely yours,

Michael McGinty, M.D.

Is That a Fact?!

Food allergies can cause histamines and other chemicals to be released into the blood stream. These chemicals can produce mild hives, swelling, and even life-threatening shock. The most common food allergies include eggs, nuts, seafood, and some fruits. Because true allergic reactions to food are rare, you should see your doctor before you restrict your diet.

JOB 112: Composed Report

A woman rushes into the office with her child, bypassing Admissions. The child obviously is having serious difficulty breathing. Neither person has an appointment, and all of the unit doctors have a full schedule of patients.

Write a one-paragraph report, entitled *Emergency Situations*, describing how you would handle this urgent situation. Refer to the Procedures Manual for the Center's policy on emergency situations. Keep in mind the urgency of this situation as you compose your answer.

JOB 113: Patient Data Files

Physicians or nurses may give necessary details for notes of patients' visits to office assistants orally. Sharp listening, note taking, and composition skills are essential for the assistant to type an accurate record of the visit.

A prescription for an ongoing medication may be refilled or renewed without an examination or checkup by the physician if the patient's medical history is known to the physician. The physician or physician's assistant will telephone the prescription to the pharmacy, with the understanding that the patient will schedule the appointment for an examination or checkup in the near future.

Several of Dr. Barnett's patients called the office today to request prescription refills. Ms. Stevens reviewed their files and telephoned the approved refills to the pharmacies. Using the information below, type a data file for each patient. Save the documents with the names *job112a*, *job112b*, and *job112c*, respectively.

Leonard Ivey; Birth Date: 5/7/59; Chief Complaint: Sore Throat; Consultation: No fever. He indicated his phlegm was clear. Westside Pharmacy was called. Refilled Keflex 250 mg (GG), 32 tablets, 1 tablet 4 x a day.

Jean McFadden; Birth Date: 7/9/32; Chief Complaint: High Blood Pressure; Consultation: Just asked to have an ongoing prescription filled. Cut-Rate Pharmacy was called. Refilled Apresoline 25 mg (GG), 60 tablets, 1 twice a day, and Slow-K 8 mEq tablets (600 mg) Geneva, 60 tablets, 1 twice a day.

Clinton Jones; Birth Date: 9/23/43; Chief Complaint: Gout; Consultation: Just asked to have ongoing prescription refilled. Lewis Pharmacy was called. Refilled Zyloprim 100 mg (GG), 60 tablets, 1 daily. Ms. Stevens reminded the patient to make an appointment for his annual physical.

JOB 114: Announcement Letter

Announcements of a general nature are often typed on letterhead.

Dr. Emerson will be leaving the Center next month. Dr. Veenstra has informed the Unit staff of Dr. Emerson's departure. She would also like to inform Dr. Emerson's patients and notify them of the transition process. Transcribe this announcement letter on Unit letterhead.

> this announcement goes to all of doctor emersons patients ... doctor emerson has accepted a position in the internal medicine unit at south mountain medical clinic ... phoenix ... arizona ... beginning the first of ... *(two months from the current month)* ... the staff and physicians at hayes medical center are sorry to see him leave ... *(Paragraph)* ... doctor larry curtis will be joining us the first of ... *(two months from the current month)* ... and will be assuming the care of doctor emersons patients ... doctor curtis has been in practice in the toledo area since nineteen eighty five ... he will be a great addition to our staff ... and will help us make the transition in our unit as smooth as possible ... *(Paragraph)* ... if you have questions or concerns about your change of physician ... please feel free to call doctor nancy veenstra ... director of internal medicine ... hayes medical center ... four one nine ... five five five ... seven eight zero zero ... extension seven eight three zero ...

JOB 115: Information Sheet

Drs. Barnett and Emerson serve on a Center-wide committee for AIDS awareness. Their objective is to write a statement concerning AIDS which will be distributed to local schools. Center and type the headings in all caps and bold with a blank line above and below. Type the rest of the statement single-spaced and use an appropriate border. Use plain paper and vertically center the job.

What Are HIV and AIDS?

HIV (Human Immunodeficiency Virus) is the virus that causes AIDS (Acquired Immune Deficiency Syndrome). HIV attacks the body's immune system, which helps keep the body healthy by fighting germs. A person with HIV can't fight the germs, and eventually the virus turns into AIDS.

(continued on next page)

Can It Be Caught at School From a Friend?

You cannot catch AIDS from everyday contact. It is not like measles or flu. If you know someone with AIDS, you can sit next to him/her, play games together, eat in the school cafeteria together, and even use the same bathroom. You can also give him or her a big hug.

How Can I Help Someone With Aids?

Be a good friend. Support and treat your friend just like your other friends who don't have AIDS. They don't like or need to be treated differently.

When Does Someone With Aids Die?

People can live for years with AIDS, but there is absolutely no cure. Scientists and medical professionals are working every day to find a cure, but until a cure is found, people will die as a result of AIDS. No one knows how long a person with AIDS will live. The most important thing you can do is help a person with AIDS live the best possible life.

Who Can I Call for Further Information?

For further information, please write or call:

Hayes Medical Center

3231 Riverside Drive

Perrysburg, OH 43551-1001

419-555-7800

Is That a Fact?!

People with high blood pressure can lower their blood pressure by making lifestyle changes. These changes include losing weight for those who are overweight and regular, aerobic exercise. Reducing salt, alcohol, and dietary fat, and increasing fruits, vegetables, and low-fat dairy foods needed for calcium, potassium, and magnesium, will also help.

The Center's Radiology Department would like you to prepare the report of Kenneth David's lumbar spine examination. Use the current date for the report and the date of the exam.

Kenneth David; Date of Birth: 10/11/50; Examination: Lumbar Spine, Pelvis; Referring Physician: Nancy Veenstra, M.D.; X Ray No.: 199232

Lumbar Spine: Examination of the lumbar spine in 5 views reveals a dextrorotoscoliosis. Degenerative changes are present in the spine. The apparent narrowing at L4-5 interspace may, in part, be related to projection. I believe this is most likely a true finding, however. A calcification in the right upper quadrant is noted. A gallstone is not excluded. Ultrasound of the gallbladder may aid. The pedicle, dorsal, and transverse processes are intact. No fracture is seen. No spondylolysis or spondylolisthesis is noted. Calcifications overlying the upper and lower portions of the right kidney are noted incidentally. On the lateral view, however, calcification is fairly far anteriorly. I doubt that this condition is due solely to calcification within the kidney. Ultrasound also would aid in evaluation of possible renal lithiasis.

Impression: Degenerative changes with dextrorotoscoliosis. Narrow L4-5 interspace. Possible gallstone; ultrasound may aid.

Pelvis: Examination of the pelvis in single AP view reveals degenerative changes and scoliosis in the low lumbar spine. The soft tissues are prominent. The pelvis appears intact. No fracture is seen. The hip joint spaces are unremarkable.

Impression: Essentially normal pelvis

John P. Boland, M.D.

Radiologist

Revise the Consultation Report if you have any errors in it. Resave it as *port10*. Print one copy for your portfolio.

Appendix

Skillbuilding

Warmups and timings are provided for each unit. The warmups, which consist of individual lines of medical terms, will help you loosen your fingers and become familiar with the terminology in each unit.

The timings will help you build speed and accuracy in typing medical documents. They contain abbreviations, numbers, symbols, and medical terminology.

Abbreviations

A list of some of the more common medical abbreviations is provided as a reference for the document processing activities. If an abbreviation is not listed, refer to a medical dictionary to determine how it should be typed.

Glossary

The Glossary defines each of the medical terms found in the *Terms to Know* sections as well as many other terms used in production jobs.

Directories

Use the staff directory of Hayes Medical Center personnel to look up professional titles, units, room numbers, and extensions. Use the patient directory to look up patients' addresses and telephone numbers.

Charts

Use the Medicines and Medical Terminology Chart to record definitions of medicines and medical terms that are not defined in the Glossary. Use the Technical Data Chart to record medical phrases or words, technical data, and abbreviations to help you remember their formats as you process the documents in this book.

Use the Job Profile Chart provided for each unit to help you keep track of the jobs that you have completed.

Admissions

WARMUP

Type each line 2 times.

```
ascites dermalgia carpal enterorrhagia axilla eupnea distal    12
flurbiprofen empiricism frenum lithiasis mastoid dehiscence    24
hypokinesis immunology oncology laxity urology trophic acne    36
```

| 1 | 2 | 3 | 4 | 5 | 6 | 7 | 8 | 9 | 10 | 11 | 12 |

TIMING

Take a 5-minute timing. Note your speed and errors.

```
    Following the intravenous administration of contrast     11
material, multiple direct coronal and axial CT images of      22
the orbits were obtained. No earlier studies were available   34
for comparison.                                               37
    There is no sign of an intracoronal or extracoronal       48
orbital mass. The extraocular muscles and orbital nerves      59
appear symmetric and within normal limits bilaterally. The    71
globes appear intact bilaterally. No osseous erosion or       82
destruction is identified.                                    88
    There is soft tissue density entirely filling the left    99
maxillary sinus and occluding the osteomeatal unit on the     111
side. When comparing the study to the exam of October 24,     122
1999, the aspect is very similar. The earlier questioned      134
deformity involving the floor of the left orbit is again      145
visualized without apparent interval change in position       156
of alignment. There is again prominent calcification seen     168
within the anterior interhemispheric fissure.                 177
    The previously related deformity of the left orbital      188
floor is again identified without significant interval        199
change with regard to position from the previous study.       210
Some soft tissue density completely filling the left          220
maxillary sinus and occluding the left osteomeatal unit       231
is still noted.                                               234
```

| 1 | 2 | 3 | 4 | 5 | 6 | 7 | 8 | 9 | 10 | 11 | 12 |

Head and Neck

WARMUP

Type each line 2 times.

```
adenoid nares endotracheal nasopharynx aphonia asymmetrical      12
cerebellum dysphagia lymphadenectomy mucosa myringotomy ala      24
otitis adenoidectomy paranasal otolaryngologist osteomeatal      36
```

| 1 | 2 | 3 | 4 | 5 | 6 | 7 | 8 | 9 | 10 | 11 | 12 |

TIMING

Take a 5-minute timing. Note your speed and errors.

```
    Ms. Lee underwent endoscopic sinus surgery in May. She        11
had been doing well; however, she developed infection with        23
green nasal drainage and still had crusting present and           34
some green drainage when irrigating. The patient has some         46
congestion, more so on the left side. The patient was on          57
Entex LA and Beconase without noticing a great deal of            68
change in her symptoms.                                           73
    The purpose of this test was to stress the status of          84
the windows, especially on the left.                              91
    The patient was placed in an examining chair in a            101
sitting position. Each nares was sprayed with 1/2% Neo-          113
Synephrine spray, followed by 4% Xylocaine spray. Cotton         124
pledgets soaked in a similar solution were placed up into        136
each nares bilaterally. After an ample amount of waiting         147
time, the pledgets were removed. The 0 degree and the 30         158
degree Storz endoscopes were inserted and used to examine        170
the nose and sinus areas.                                        175
    This patient had slightly more edema on the left. The        186
patient had some edema at the uncinate area and perhaps          197
granulation or simply swollen tissue. The ethmoid area was       209
well visualized and found to be very clean of granulation        221
and very exonerated with no inflammation or drainage.            231
```

| 1 | 2 | 3 | 4 | 5 | 6 | 7 | 8 | 9 | 10 | 11 | 12 |

UNIT 3

Cardiovascular

WARMUP

Type each line 2 times.

```
aneurysmal atherectomy bradycardia ectatic echocardiography     12
angioplasty exertional hemoglobin prothrombin nitroglycerin     24
sodium arrhythmia cholesterol reconstructive hyperlipidemia     36

| 1 | 2 | 3 | 4 | 5 | 6| 7 | 8 | 9 |10| 11 | 12 |
```

TIMING

Take a 5-minute timing. Note your speed and errors.

```
     Mrs. Alonzo was seen in followup after hospitalization     11
for unstable angina culminating in transfer to Ohio Clinic      23
for coronary angioplasty. This was a technically demanding      35
procedure as the patient experienced a localized dissection     47
which appeared to threaten but never progressed to total        58
occlusion. It subsequently stabilized angiographically,         71
and the patient was observed for several days. She then         82
underwent a negative stress cardiolite scan to a level of       93
12 MET., a peak heart rate of 153 per minute, with no           104
evidence for infarction or ischemia. In the interval since      116
her discharge, she has been asymptomatic. Of interest were      128
two types of discomfort: (1) upper chest burning, probably      140
angina that was experienced during balloon inflation, and       151
(2) an epigastric burning, resulting when flat in the           162
evening and postprandially, felt to be reflux. The patient      174
has now been asymptomatic in regards to the latter on           185
Tagamet.                                                        186
     On examination, see vitals above. The patient's lungs      197
were clear. Her heart tones were regular. There was no          208
audible cardiac gallop or murmur. Extremities revealed no       220
edema and there were good peripheral pulses. An EKG             230
reveals sinus rhythm—small, inferior Q waves without any        242
change from newer hospital or other tracings.                   251

| 1 | 2 | 3 | 4 | 5 | 6| 7 | 8 | 9 |10| 11 | 12 |
```

Plastic Surgery

WARMUP

Type each line 2 times.

ulcerate vasospasm thorac otalgia pruritus phlebitis flexor   12
metastasis idiopathic reocclude seroma erythema ventricular   24
cerebellar cheilorrhaphy desensitize abrasions aerola nodes   36

| 1 | 2 | 3 | 4 | 5 | 6| 7 | 8 | 9 |10 | 11 | 12 |

TIMING

Take a 5-minute timing. Note your speed and errors.

Mr. Longworth is a 38-year-old male who works for an   11
automobile manufacturer. During the last 10 months, he at   22
first noted some tingling in his fingertips; then, later,   34
pain that began to radiate up his right arm. The patient   45
uses wrenches and does a repetitive type work. At first,   57
his physician placed his wrist in some splints. His physician 69
also recommended that Mr. Longworth take time off from his   81
job and undergo physical therapy. The patient complied with   97
these recommendations. Mr. Longworth was given some Motrin   104
and some other anti-inflammatories of which he is unable to   116
remember the names. Mr. Longworth states that the splints   128
helped for a while, but when he started working again, his   140
symptoms got worse. At this point, even with the splints,   151
he still frequently has difficulty getting a good night's   163
rest. The patient says that when he drives or when he reads   175
a paper at night, his right hand goes to sleep.   185

Physical examination shows a well-developed 38-year-   195
old male whose right hand shows no trophic changes. Tinel's   207
and phalen's signs are positive. This right-handed patient   219
has a good pulse. His strength registers 260 on the right   231
and 300 on the left. Mr. Longworth denies any history of   242
diabetes mellitus or thyroid disease, and states that he is   254
allergic to penicillin.   259

| 1 | 2 | 3 | 4 | 5 | 6| 7 | 8 | 9 |10 | 11 | 12 |

Allergy/Immunology

WARMUP

Type each line 2 times.

```
medial maxillary aeroallergen pustule dyspnea sebopsoriasis       12
hyposensitization immunotherapy intertrigo neurodermatitis        24
bronchus surgery prednisone claudication excoriations pedis       36
```

| 1 | 2 | 3 | 4 | 5 | 6 | 7 | 8 | 9 |10 |11 | 12 |

TIMING

Take a 5-minute timing. Note your speed and errors.

```
      The patient has severe allergic rhinitis. At times he       11
has had symptoms of superimposed infection involving both         23
upper and lower airways.                                          28
      A record of wheezing is noted, occurring at the age of      39
5. Theophylline sprinkle was prescribed, but it was not           50
tolerated. A history of bronchospasm induced by exercise or       62
allergen exposure is absent. Whether he has asthma or not         74
is an undecided issue. T&A at the age of 5 appeared to            85
improve edisodes of purulent rhinitis. A sibling has both         96
asthma and rhinitis. The patient's medical system review is      108
negative.                                                         110
      Physical examination of this patient reveals a male        121
normotensive Caucasian in the 75th percentile of weight and      133
in the 90th percentile of height. He has allergic shiners.       144
An inspection of the eardrums by pneumoscopy was normal.         156
Nasal airflow was markedly diminished, and the nasal mucosa      168
was pale and wet. There was brownish-green mucous caked in       180
the nasal vestibules. Marked cobblestoning and edema of the      192
pharynx were present. Cervical glands were not enlarged.         203
The heart and lung examination was normal.                       212
      Allergy skin tests by prick puncture were positive to      223
dust, mites, cockroach, cat, dog, and ragweed pollen. The        234
remainder of comprehensive allergy tests by prick puncture       246
and introdermal were negative.                                   252
```

| 1 | 2 | 3 | 4 | 5 | 6 | 7 | 8 | 9 |10 |11 | 12 |

UNIT 6

Urology

WARMUP

Type each line 2 times.

```
fibroid obstruction prostate panandoscope dysuria surrogate      12
cystoscopy incontinence fibrillation aspirated trabeculated      24
retroperitoneum occlusion catheter micturition erythromycin      36

|  1  |  2  |  3  |  4  |  5  |  6  |  7  |  8  |  9  | 10  | 11  | 12  |
```

TIMING

Take a 5-minute timing. Note your speed and errors.

```
     The patient was observed in the ICU. She was treated      11
by Dr. Wilkinson and associates. She had been on long-term      23
antihypertensive therapy and needed supervision of her          34
medications and fluid management. Dr. Dill was in charge of      46
her hypertension and observation of her renal function. By      57
5-14-99 her GI function had returned and she was moved to       69
her room. Her blood pressure remained easily managed. Her       81
wound remained unremarkable. By 5-15-99 the patient was         92
ambulating and eating a normal diet. Her blood pressures       103
were in the 170/90 range. She was discharged home on Bumex     115
1 mg b.i.d., which is a reduction of 1 Bumex pill a day        126
relative to admission.                                         131
     She was discharged on Lanoxin 0.125 mg q.d., Norvasc 5    142
Mg q.d., which was a new medicine, Capoten 50 mg b.i.d.,       153
K-Dur 20 mg b.i.d., Mevacor 20 mg q HS., Proventil inhaler     165
2 puffs q.i.d., Zantac 150 mg b.i.d., and Orudis 25 mg         176
b.i.d. Her Verelan 240 mg q.d. was discontinued. At the        187
time of her discharge her final hemoglobin was 10.6, final     199
white count 6,500. Final discharge BUN 11, creatinine 1.1,     211
final potassium 4.0.  Portable chests were done during her     223
hospitalization. She formed a right lower lobe infiltrate,     234
which resolved with Timentin therapy. EKGs showed atrial       246
fibrillation with an old anteroseptal MI and some ST-T wave    258
abnormalities.                                                 260

|  1  |  2  |  3  |  4  |  5 |  6 |  7  |  8  |  9  | 10  | 11  | 12  |
```

Surgery

WARMUP

Type each line 2 times.

hepatosplenomegaly internal auscultation granuloma ganglion   12
cholecystectomy malleoli femur fibroperitoneal enterotomies   24
pneumoperitoneum palpation laparotomy adenopathy hemostasis   36

| 1 | 2 | 3 | 4 | 5 | 6| 7 | 8 | 9 | 10 | 11 | 12 |

TIMING

Take a 5-minute timing. Note your speed and errors.

The patient is a 50-year-old white male who recently   11
had an excision of multiple lipomatous-like lesions of the   23
right chest, flank, and right medial thigh. The pathology   34
report on the other specimens revealed simple lipoma, but   46
the specimen of the right medial thigh was revealed to be a   58
Grade III malignant fibrous histiocytoma. As it was excised   70
in a fashion consistent with lipoma, the tumor was noted to   82
come to the margin of resection. The pathology was also   93
discussed with the patient, and the pathology results were   105
reviewed with University of Michigan Pathology, which made   117
the diagnosis. The patient was presented with the surgical   128
options and wished to proceed with wide re-excision of the   140
wound. Consultation was made with Dr. Knight, who felt that   152
postoperative radiation therapy would be the most suitable   163
adjuvant therapy.   167

Because of the necessity for wide re-excision of the   178
area and for particularly wide re-excision because of a   189
postoperative wound hematoma that occurred in the area, a   201
referral was made to Dr. Lee to participate in a combined   212
procedure for closure or coverage of the wound after the   224
wide excision of the area. There are risks, benefits, and   235
potential complications of surgery; these were discussed   247
by Dr. Lee along with the surgical options at present.   258

| 1 | 2 | 3 | 4 | 5 | 6| 7 | 8 | 9 | 10 | 11 | 12 |

Oncology

WARMUP

Type each line 2 times.

monogram medullary laxity lipomas malleolar keratoacanthoma   12

trocars supine carcinoma chemotherapy remission polypectomy   24

induration radiation mammogram melanoma ecchymoses palpable   36

| 1 | 2 | 3 | 4 | 5 | 6 | 7 | 8 | 9 | 10 | 11 | 12 |

TIMING

Take a 5-minute timing. Note your speed and errors.

This 77-year-old woman had surgical treatment of a   10

vulvar cancer in the recent past. This required bilateral   22

groin lymph node dissections, and likely radiation therapy   34

is a consideration.   38

During planning for treatment of her vulvar cancer, a   49

CT scan was performed which suggested a right kidney tumor.   61

Subsequently, an angiogram was done, which showed a large   72

right kidney with a relatively avascular mass in the right   84

upper kidney area. There is a small left kidney with a   95

preocclusive non-stenosis in the left renal artery.   105

She was facing partial or total right nephrectomy and   116

was seen for advice on treatment for treating her left   127

renal artery stenosis. It was felt the renal artery lesion   139

was technically dilatable. She elected a left renal artery   151

angioplasty which was compounded by a distal dissection   162

beyond the plane of cosmetically successful angioplasty.   174

This dissection was watched for a short period of time on   185

the angiogram table with repeated films. The dissection   196

worsened and flow decreased to the left kidney.   206

The patient was taken to the operating room urgently   217

on 5-21-99 and had a left aorto-renal bypass using 6 mm   228

thin wall Gore-Tex.   232

| 1 | 2 | 3 | 4 | 5 | 6 | 7 | 8 | 9 | 10 | 11 | 12 |

Dermatology

WARMUP

*Type each line 2
times.*

```
lichenification eczematous recalcitrant varicella cheilitis    12
molluscum premenopausal edematous hematoma lichen urticatus    24
salicysalicylic acid antecubital dermatology hyperkeratotic    36
```

| 1 | 2 | 3 | 4 | 5 | 6 | 7 | 8 | 9 | 10 | 11 | 12 |

TIMING

*Take a 5-minute
timing. Note your
speed and errors.*

```
     Mary Rainey was in the office on July 11, 1999, with      11
the chief complaint of drug eruption, supposedly resulting     23
from one component of erythema multiform major, that of        34
Stevens-Johnson syndrome.                                      39
     Examination reveals a morbilliform-type eruption over     50
the arms, legs, trunk, and entire body. Oral ulcerations       61
were noted, and the patient stated she was very pruritic.      73
She stated that the eruption occurred after EES. There is      85
some question as to her taking amoxicillin. Also, it might     96
be that erythromycin was the culprit, although amoxicillin    108
could not be ruled out.                                       113
     The patient was given an injection of Depo-Medrol 60     124
mg IM, started on prednisone 3 every morning x 5 days, 2      135
every morning x 5 days, and 1 every morning x 5 days, to be   147
weaned over a 15-day period. She was advised to watch very    159
closely for any changes. If she is not moving fluids or is    171
having any complications, she should return.                  180
     The patient called over the weekend; she complained      190
about a slight rash on her lips. She was advised to rub       202
Vaseline on her lips. The patient was in the office today.    213
She was approximately 50% improved. She was advised to take   225
cool showers and no aspirin.                                  231
```

| 1 | 2 | 3 | 4 | 5 | 6 | 7 | 8 | 9 | 10 | 11 | 12 |

Internal Medicine

WARMUP

Type each line 2 times.

urinalysis leukocytes apraxia hemostat morphology avascular   12
demyelination scoliosis hydronephrosis hemoptysis dysphagia   24
thromboid dextrorotation dysfunction extraocular epithelium   36

| 1 | 2 | 3 | 4 | 5 | 6 | 7 | 8 | 9 | 10 | 11 | 12 |

TIMING

Take a 5-minute timing. Note your speed and errors.

Examination of the lumbar spine in 5 views reveals a   11
dextrorotoscoliosis. Degenerative changes are present in   22
the spine. The apparent narrowing at L4-5 interspace may,   34
in part, be related to projection. This is likely a true   45
conclusion; however, a calcification in the right upper   56
quadrant is noted. A gallstone is not excluded. Ultrasound   68
of the gallbladder may be of help. The pedicle, dorsal, and   80
transverse processes are intact. No fracture is seen. No   92
spondylolysis or spondylolisthesis is seen. Calcifications   103
overlying the upper and lower portions of the right kidney   115
are noted in passing. On the lateral view, calcification is   127
fairly far anteriorly. It is doubtful that this condition   139
is due solely to calcification within the kidney. Having   150
an ultrasound also would aid in evaluation of possible   161
renal lithiasis.   165

There also appears to be a lot of degenerative changes   176
with dextrorotoscoliosis and narrow L4-5 interspace. Again,   188
ultrasound may aid in determining if gallstone is possible.   200

Examination of the pelvis in single AP view reveals   210
degenerative changes and scoliosis in the lower lumbar   221
spine. The soft tissues are prominent. The pelvis appears   233
intact. No fracture is seen. The hip joint spaces are not   245
remarkable.   247

Essentially, the pelvis is normal.   254

| 1 | 2 | 3 | 4 | 5 | 6 | 7 | 8 | 9 | 10 | 11 | 12 |

ABBREVIATIONS

A sample of common abbreviations is given in the following chart. For a complete listing, refer to a medical dictionary. Many abbreviations come from Latin words; usually they are typed in all capital letters or lowercase letters with periods. It is important to type the periods in medical abbreviations, especially if without the periods, the abbreviation would spell another word, for example, b.i.d. without the periods is the word *bid*.

A

a., ante.	before	aa	equal parts of
AB	abort, miscarry	ABC	airway, breathing, and
ABD	abdomen		circulation
ACG	angiocardiogram	a.c.	before meals
ad lib.	as much as needed	a.d.	up to
A-fib	atrial fibrillation	A-tach	atrial tachycardia
agit	shake, stir	AIDS	acquired immodeficiency
alt. hor.	alternate hours		syndrome
alt. nor.	alternate nights	alt. dieb.	alternate days
AMA	American Medical Association	AMI	acute myocardial infarction
	against medical advice	ant.	anterior
amt.	amount	anat.	anatomy
ANA	American Nurses' Association	ARC	AIDS related complex
AOA	American Orthopsychiatric Association	ASHD	arteriosclerotic heart disease
	American Osteopathic Association	AV	atrioventricular
	American Optometric Asociation	AVF	augmented
ASA	acetysalicylic acid (aspirin)		electrocardiographic lead from the left foot

B

b.i.d.	twice a day	bilat.	bilateral
BM	bowel movement	BMR	basal metabolic rate
BP	blood pressure	BS	blood sugar; breath sounds
BUN	blood urea nitrogen		

C

c or /c	with	CA	carcinoma; cardiac arrest; coronary artery; chronological age
Ca.	cancer		
CAD	coronary artery disease		
CAT	computerized axial tomography scan	C-1, etc.	first cervical vertebrae
cbc	complete blood count	ca.	calorie
CC	chief complaint	caps.	capsule
CDC	Centers for Disease Control	cc.	cubic centimeter
CHF	congestive heart failure	CCU	coronary care unit
CMS	circulation, movement, sensation	CHD	coronary heart disease
CNS	central nervous system	CHI	closed head injury
comp	compound	cm.	centimeter
COPD	choronic obstructive pulmonary disease	Co.	cobalt
COR	the heart; relating to the heart	contra	against
CPE	complete physical exam	C/O	complaining of
CRNA	Certified Registered Nurse Anesthetist	CPR	cardiopulmonary resuscitation
CT	computerized tomography		

		CSF	cerebrospinal fluid
		CVA	cerebrovascular accident (stroke)

D

DB	decibel—a measurement of sound	D&C	dilation and curettage
DC	discontinue	d.d.	let it be given to
dil.	dilute	Div.	to be divided
DNA	deoxyribonucleic acid	DNR	do not resuscitate
DOA	dead on arrival	Dos.	doses
dr	dram	DSD	double starting dose
DTR	deep tendon reflex	Dx	diagnosis

E

ECG	electrocardiogram	ECT	electroconvulsive therapy
EEG	electroencephalogram	EENT	eyes, ears, nose, and throat
EKG	electrocardiogram	elix.	elixir
EMG	electromyogram	ENT	ears, nose, and throat
EOM	extraocular movement; extraocular muscle	ER	emergency room
et.	and	exp.	expiratory
ext. or extr.	extract, or extremities		

F

F.	Fahrenheit	f. or ft.	make; let there be made
FBAO	foreign body airway obstruction	fl. oz.	fluid ounce
Fl. or fl.	fluid		
Fx.	fracture		

G

g. or gm	gram	garg.	gargle
GI	gastrointestinal	gr.	grain
GSW	gunshot wound	gt.	drop
gtt.	drops	GU	genitourinary
guttat.	drop by drop		

H

h.	hour	HA	headache
Hb or Hgb.	hemoglobin	HDL	high-density lipoprotein
HEENT	head, ears, eyes, nose, and throat	HMO	health maintenance organization
HPI	history of present illness/injury	h.s.	before bedtime (hour of sleep)
HTN	hypertension	Hx.	history

I

ICU	intensive care unit	Ig	Immunoglobulin
IM	intramuscularly by intramuscular injection	inj.	injection; to be injected
IOP	intraocular pressure	IQ	intelligence quotient
IV	intravenously; by intravenous injection		

J

JVD	jugular vein distention		

K

K.	potassium	kg	kilogram
KUB	kidney, ureter, and bladder	kV	kilovolt

L

l	liter	LAD	leukocyte adhesion deficiency
L&A	light and accommodation (reaction of pupils of eyes)	LAX	not tense, firm, or rigid; loose, slack, vague, unconfined, unrestrained
LDL	low-density lipoproteins	LDH	lactate dehydrogenase
LLQ	left lower quandrant		
LOC	loss/level of consciousness	L1	first lumbar vertebra (L1-L5)
LS	lung sounds	LMP	last menstrual period
		LPN	licensed practical nurse
		LUQ	left upper quandrant

M

MCA	motorcycle accident	M. or m.	mix, median, meter, milli
mEq.	milliequivalent	mcgm.	microgram
mid.	middle	MI	myocardial infarction
ml	milliliter	mg	milligram
MRI	magnetic resonance imaging	mm.	millimeter
MUGA	a noninvasive test used to detect and evaluate heart muscle function before and after exercise	MS	multiple sclerosis
		MVA	motor vehicle accident

N

N&V	nausea and vomiting	NAD	no acute distress
neg./−	negative	NG	nasogastric
NKA	no known allergies	Noct. or noct.	night or at night
NPN	nonprotein nitrogen	NPO	nothing by mouth
NSR	normal sinus rhythm		

O

O	oxygen	OB	obstetrics
OD	overdose	O.D.	right eye
o.h.	every hour	O.L.	left eye
o.m.	every morning	o.n.	every night
OR	operating room	os	bone

P

p.	after	P.	pulse
p.a.	in equal parts	PAC	premature atrial contraction
palp.	palpated, palpatation	PAT	paroxysmal atrial tradycardia
PBI	protein-bound iodine	p.c.	after meals, after food
PE	physical exam; pulmonary embolism	ped.	pediatric, pediatrics

PERRLA	pupils equal, round, reactive to light and accommodation; used to note results of an eye test		PET	positron emission tomography
PG	pregnant, pregnancy		pH	hydrogen ion concentration
PID	pelvic inflammatory disease		pil.	pill
PMH	past medical history		PMI	point of maximal impulse
PND	post nasal drip		P.O. or p.o.	by mouth, orally
PO$_2$	oxygen partial pressure		pos./+	positive
post.	posterior		p.r.n.	according to circumstances; as required; as needed; whenever necessary
Pt.	patient			
PTCA	percutaneous transliminal coronary angioplasty		PTA	plasma thromboplastin antecedent; physical therapy assistant
			PTT	partial thromboplastin time
			PVC	premature ventricular contraction

Q

q.	every		q.a.m.	every morning
q.d.	one time daily, every day		q.i. h.	every 4 hours
q.h.	every hour		q.i.d.	four times a day (not at night)
q. noc.	every night		q.n.s.	quantity not sufficient
q.o.d.	every other day		q.p.m.	every night
q.s.	quantity sufficient		q.2 h.	every 2 hours

R

R	respirations		RBC	red blood (cell) count
REM	rapid eye movements		rep.	let it be repeated
RLQ	right lower quandrant		RNP	ribonucleoprotein
R/O	rule out		ROM	range of motion
RUQ	right upper quadrant		Rx	treatment; take (recipe); prescription

S

s or /s	without		S1	first sacral vetebra (S1-S5)
sat.	saturated		S-brady	sinus bradycardia
S-tach or SVT	sinus tachycardia		Sig.	let it be labeled; give directions on prescription
SL	sublingual		SO	standing order
SOB	shortness of breath		sol.	solution
SQ or subq.	subcutaneous		ss.	one-half
ST	sinus tachycardia		stat.	immediately
SVT	supraventricular tachycardia		Sx.	symptoms
syr.	syrup			

T

T&A	tonsils and adenoids		tab.	tablet
tach.	tachycardia		TB	tuberculosis
TBSA	total body surface area		TIA	transient ischemic attack
t.i.d.	three times a day		TKO	to keep open

T1	first thoracic vertebra (T1-T12)		TPA	tissue plasminogen activator
tr. or tinct.	tincture		troc.	lozenge
TSH	thyroid-stimulating hormone		tsp.	teaspoon

U

u.	unit		URI	upper respiratory infection
UTI	urinary tract infection		UV	ultraviolet

V

V	volt		var.	variety
VD	venereal disease		V-fib.	ventricular fibrillation
V-tach	ventricular tachycardia		VO	verbal order
VS	vital signs			

W

WBC	white blood (cell) count		WNL	within normal limits
wt	weight			

GLOSSARY

abrasion   A scraping or rubbing away of a surface.

acanthosis   A thickening of the skin, as in eczema and psoriasis.

acne   A breakout of pimples.

adenocarcinoma   Glandular cancer.

adenoid   Like or resembling a gland.

adenoidectomy   Removal of the adenoids.

adenopathy   Swelling or morbid enlargement of the lymph nodes.

aeroallergen   A foreign substance in the air that can cause an allergic response in the body but is harmful only to some people.

aeruginosa   Bacteria.

ala   A piece of bone on each side of the upper part of the nose.

allergy   Exaggerated reaction (sneezing, itching, breathing problems, skin rashes) to substances, situations, or physical states that are without comparable effects on the average individual.

alveolus   A small saclike structure.

amoxicillin   A type of penicillin taken by mouth.

anastomosis   An opening or connection between two vessels or organs.

aneurysmal   Relating to an aneurysm.

angioplasty   Reconstruction of a blood vessel.

antecubital   At the bend of the elbow on the inside of the arm.

antrostomy   The formation of an opening into any antrum (nearly closed cavity).

aphonia   A defect in which the patient is not able to make normal speech sounds.

apraxia   Loss of ability to do simple or routine acts.

areola   A small space or cavity; a circular area of different color surrounding a skin lesion with pus.

arrhythmia   Any change in the normal pattern of the heart.

arthritis   Any inflammation of the joints, marked by pain and swelling.

ascites   An abnormal pooling of fluid containing large amounts of protein and other cells in the abdominal cavity.

aspirated   Fluids were withdrawn.

asymmetrical   Unequal in size or shape.

ataxia   An inability to coordinate movements.

atherectomy   Removal of deposits from the lining of an artery.

auscultation   Listening to sounds made by the various body structures as a diagnostic method.

avascular   An area not receiving a sufficient supply of blood; can be the result of a blood clot or the intentional stopping of blood flow during surgery.

axilla   The underside of the shoulder between the upper part of the arm and the side of the chest; armpit.

bradycardia   An abnormal condition in which the heart contracts steadily but at a rate of less than 60 beats per minute.

bronchi   One of the two subdivisions of the trachea serving to convey air to and from the lungs.

bronchitis Inflammation of the bronchi.

bronchus Another term for bronchi.

Capoten A drug prescribed for high blood pressure or congestive heart failure.

carcinoma Malignant cancer occurring in skin, intestines, lungs, prostate glands, or breasts.

cardiolite An isotope used in cardiac stress testing.

cardiopulmonary Referring to the heart and lungs.

cardiovascular Referring to the heart and blood vessels.

carpal Referring to the wrist.

catheter A tubular instrument used to allow passage of fluid from or into a body cavity.

catheterization Placement of a catheter into a body cavity or organ to add or remove fluid.

cerebellar Referring to a part of the brain.

cerebellum A part of the brain located at the base of the skull behind the brain stem.

cervical Referring to the neck.

cervix Any neck-like structure.

cheilitis Inflammation of the lip.

cheilorrhaphy Plastic surgery of the lips.

chemotherapy Treatment of disease by means of chemical substances or drugs.

chiropractic A system of therapeutics which attempts to restore normal function of the body by its manipulation.

cholecystectomy Surgical removal of the gallbladder.

cholesterol Substance found in animal fats and oils, egg yolk, and the human body.

claudication A pain in the legs with cramps in the calves caused by poor circulation of blood in the legs.

collagen The major protein of the white fibers of connective tissue, cartilage, and bone.

congestion Abnormal collection of fluid in an organ or body area.

contractility The ability of the heart to contract when properly stimulated.

cryptic Hidden.

cystoscopy Inspection of the interior of the bladder by means of a cystoscope.

dehiscence Separation of a surgical cut.

demyelination Destruction of the covering of a nerve.

dermalgia Skin pain.

dermatology A branch of science dealing with the skin, its structure, functions, and diseases.

desensitize To make a person insensitive to any of the various foreign substances that might cause an allergic reaction.

dextrorotation A turning or twisting to the right.

diaphoresis Profuse sweating that occurs with a fever, physical exertion, exposure to heat, or stress.

distal Away from the point of origin.

dorsal Relating to or situated near or on the back.

dorsal dysfunction The inability of the dorsum or back to function normally.

dorsal ectatic Dilation of a posterior tubular structure.

dorsal pedis The back or upper surface of the foot.

dorsum Another word for back.

dysfunction   Impaired or abnormal functioning.

dysphagia   Difficulty in swallowing commonly linked to blockage or motor disorders of the esophagus.

dysplasia   Abnormal growth or development of the body's tissues or organs.

dyspnea   A shortness of breath or difficulty in breathing.

dysuria   Painful or difficult urination.

ecchymosis   A purplish patch caused by seepage of blood into the skin.

echocardiography   The use of ultrasound to study the heart to diagnose problems.

ectatic   Relating to or marked by dilation or expansion.

eczematous   Marked by or resembling eczema.

edematous   Afflicted with edema.

electronystagmogram   A test of the balance system to determine if the disorder is peripheral or central.

emesis   Vomiting.

empiricism   A form of therapy based on personal experiences, such as trial and error and the experiences of others in the practice.

endarterectomy   A method of removing the core of an artery that has become thickened by fatty deposits.

endocarditis   Inflammation within the heart.

endotracheal   Within or through the windpipe.

enterorrhagia   Hemorrhage from the intestine.

enterostomies   Incisions into the intestines which produce a small hole in the abdomen through which the intestines are emptied.

epistaxis   Bleeding from the nose.

epithelium   The covering of the organs of the body, including the lining of vessels.

erythema   Redness or swelling of the skin or mucous membranes.

erythromycin   An antibiotic used to treat many bacterial infections, particularly infections that cannot be treated with penicillins.

ethmoid   Resembling a sieve.

eupnea   Normal breathing.

excoriations   Injuries to the surface of the skin or other parts of the body caused by scratching or scraping.

exertional   With laborious or perceptible effort.

extraocular   Outside the eye.

fasciectomy   Excision of strips of the fibrous tissue enveloping the body beneath the skin.

femoral   Referring to the thigh.

femur   The long bone of the thigh.

fiberoptics   Process by which an internal organ or space can be viewed, using glass or plastic fibers that reflect a magnified image.

fibrillation   Rapid contractions or twitching of musculary fibrils, but not the muscle as a whole.

fibrocystic   Pertaining to or characterized by the presence of fiberocysts.

fibroid   Resembling or composed of fibers or fibrous tissue.

fibroperitoneal Related to the tissue that lines the abdominal cavity and covers most of the viscera.

flexor A muscle, the action of which is to flex a joint.

fluoroscope A device used for immediate showing of an X-ray image.

flurbiprofen A drug prescribed for rheumatoid arthritis and osteoarthritis.

frenum A restraining portion or structure.

ganglion A knot or a knotlike mass.

gestation The period of time from the fertilization of the egg until birth.

granulomatous Having the characteristics of a granuloma (nodular inflammatory lesion).

hematoma A collection of blood that has escaped from the vessels and become trapped in the tissues of the skin or in an organ.

hematuria Abnormal amount of blood in the urine.

hemoglobin A complex, red respiratory protein compound in the blood that carries oxygen to the cells and carbon dioxide away from the cells.

hemoptysis Coughing up of blood from the respiratory tract.

hemostasis The arrest of bleeding.

hemostat An instrument or medicine for stopping bleeding.

hepatosplenomegaly Enlargement of the liver or spleen.

hydronephrosis Swelling of the pelvis by urine that cannot flow past a blockage in a ureter.

hyperkeratosis Formation of skin overgrowth.

hyperkeratotic Characterized by increased growth and thickening of the outer skin cells.

hyperlipidemia An excess of fats or lipids in the blood.

hypertrophic Characterized by an increase in the bulk of a part or an organ caused by an increase in the size of the cells rather than an increase in the number of cells; not due to a tumor.

hypokinesis Hypomotility; diminished or slow movement.

hyposensitization Reduction of sensitivity to an allergen.

idiopathic Without a known cause.

immunology Science concerned with the body's resistance to disease.

immunotherapy A special treatment for allergies.

incontinence Inability to prevent discharge of excretions, especially urine or feces.

induration Process of becoming extremely firm or hard.

influenza A highly contagious infection, usually of the lungs, caused by a virus and transmitted by airborne particles.

inguinal Of or pertaining to the groin.

inspiratory Of or pertaining to the act of breathing in.

internal Away from the surface; situated inside the body.

intertrigo An irritation of opposing skin surfaces caused by friction.

intraperitoneal Within the abdominal cavity.

invasive Marked by a tendency to spread.

ischemia Poor blood supply to an organ or a part, often marked by pain and organ dysfunction.

keratoacanthoma   A rapidly growing tumor usually occurring on exposed areas of the skin; a noncancerous flesh-colored pimple that disappears on its own within 4 to 6 months.

kinesalgia   Pain on motion or movement.

laparoscopic   A minimally invasive surgical technique using a fiberoptic instrument.

laparotomy   Incision into the loin.

laryngitis   Inflammation of the larynx.

laxity   Pertaining to relaxed or loose bowels.

lesions   Wounds or injuries.

leukocytes   White blood cells.

lichen urticatus   Bug bites.

lichenification   A thickening and hardening of the skin.

lipomas   Benign tumors of fatty tissues.

lithiasis   The formation of stones from mineral salts in the hollow organs or ducts of the body.

living will   A document in which the signer requests to be allowed to die rather than be kept alive by artificial means if disabled beyond a reasonable expectation of recovery.

lymphadenectomy   Surgical removal of one or more lymph glands.

lymphocytes   Two kinds of small white blood cells.

lymphoma   Obsolete term for malignancy.

malignant   Tending to become worse and possibly cause death.

malleolar   Concerning a rounded bony structure such as the bump on each side of the ankle.

malleoli   Plural form of the rounded, bony prominences such as those on each side of the ankle joint.

mammogram   The record produced by mammography.

mammography   Examination of the breast by means of X-rays, ultrasound, and nuclear magnetic resonance used for screening and diagnosing diseases of the breast.

mastoid   Referring to a portion of the temporal bone of the skull.

maxillary   Relating to the maxilla, or upper jaw.

medial   Relating to the middle or center.

medullary   Relating to the soft marrow in the center of a part; the middle of the brain.

melanoma   A mole which has become malignant.

metastasis   The process by which tumor cells are spread to distant parts of the body.

micturition   Urination.

molluscum   Any skin disease marked by soft, rounded masses or nodes.

monogram   Treatise on a subject or particular part of a subject.

morphology   The study of the physical shape and size of a specimen, plant, or animal.

mucosa   Mucous membranes.

multifocal   Relating to many starting points of a disease process; many points where light rays meet after passing through a convex lens.

myelogram   An X-ray film of the spinal cord taken after the injection of a dye.

myocardial   Pertaining to the muscular tissue of the heart.

myotasis   Stretching of a muscle.

myringotomy   Surgical opening of the eardrum to relieve pressure or release pus from the middle ear.

nares   The openings in the nose that allow the passage of air to the throat and lungs during breathing.

nasopharyngolaryngoscope   An instrument, often of fiberoptic type, used to visualize the upper airways and nasopharynx.

nasopharynx   One of the three parts of the throat, behind the nose and reaching from the back of the nasal opening to the soft palate.

neuritis   Inflammation of a nerve.

neurodermatitis   An itching skin disorder seen in anxious, nervous patients.

nevus   A colored skin spot that is usually harmless but may become cancerous.

nitroglycerin   The generic name of a drug used to treat attacks of angina pectoria that are often present in various forms of heart disease.

nodes   Knobs, knuckles, or finger joints; masses of tissue.

normocephalic   Having a head of medium length.

nystagmus   Involuntary, rhythmic movements of the eyes back and forth, up and down, around, or mixed.

obstetrician   Physician specializing in the care of women during pregnancy and childbirth.

obstruction   Blockage or clogging.

occipital   Relating to bone in the back of the head.

occlusion   Act of closing or state of being closed.

oncology   The study of tumors.

organomegaly   Enlargement of an internal organ.

ossicles   Small bones of the inner ear.

osteomeatal   Pertaining to a swollen or shaggy opening to the maxillary and ethmoid sinuses, seen in the larynx.

osteopath   A practitioner of the school of medicine which states that the functional and structural interdependence of the human body are essential to the maintenance of health.

otalgia   Earache.

otitis media   Swelling or infection of the middle ear, a common disease of childhood.

otolaryngological   Relating to the diagnosis and treatment of disorders of the ear, nose, and throat.

otolaryngologist   One who specializes in the study of the ear and throat by the combination of the specialties of otology and laryngology.

palmar   Referring to the palm of the hand.

palpable   Perceptible to touch; capable of being palpated.

palpated   Used the hands or fingers to examine.

palpation   Examination with hands.

panendoscope   An instrument for inspection of the urethra or bladder.

paranasal   Near or alongside the nose.

paroxysms   Marked rises in symptoms.

pectoral   Pertaining to the chest area.

pectoris   The plural of pectus, which means the chest.

pediatrician   A physician who specializes in the diagnosis of diseases of children.

pedis   Feet.

pedunculated   Attached by a narrow stalk.

percutaneous   Done through the skin, as a biopsy.

pharyngitis   A swelling or infection of the throat, usually causing symptoms of a sore throat.

phlebitis   Inflammation of a vein.

pneumococcal   Referring to bacteria of the pneumococcus group.

pneumoperitoneum   Presence of gas in abdominal cavity.

polypectomy   Excision of a polyp.

postpartum   After childbirth.

prandial   Referring to a meal.

prednisone   A hormone used to treat severe swelling and to stop the body from having an immune response to an allergic substance.

premenopausal   Relating to the period of time preceding menopause.

Procardia   A trademark for a calcium channel blocker.

prostate   A chestnut-shaped body surrounding the beginning of the urethra in the male.

prostatectomy   Removal of a part or all of the prostate.

prothrombin   A blood plasma protein that forms thrombin, which causes clotting of whole blood.

pruritus   The symptom of itching, a feeling that makes someone want to scratch.

pustular bullae   Small blisters.

pustules   Small blisters that usually have pus.

pyelorenal   Pertaining to the basin-like or cup-shaped cavity of the kidneys.

pyrethrum   Any of several chrysanthemums, often a source of insecticides.

radiation   The art or condition of diverging in all directions from a center; used for treatment or diagnosis of disease.

recalcitrant   Not responsive to treatment.

reconstructive   The process of rebuilding or reconstructing; to put as it was before by means of surgery.

referral   To give a patient the name of a medical specialist.

remission   Abatement or lessening of severity of the symptoms of a disease.

reocclude   Reoccurrence of closing or bringing together, as in an artery.

reperfusion   The reestablishment of blood flow.

restenose   The plural of restenosis.

restenosis   The reoccurrence of a condition marked by a tightening or narrowing of an opening or passageway as in a heart valve or vessel.

retroperitoneum   Space between the stomach and intestine wall partly covered by the lining (peritoneum) and muscles and bones of the posterior abdominal wall.

rhinitis   Inflammation of the mucous membranes of the nose, with a nasal discharge.

rhinoscopy   The examination of the nasal passages to inspect the mucosa and detect swelling or defects.

salicysalicylic acid   Salsalate; a combination of two molecules of salicylic acid in ester-linkage which acts as an anti-inflammatory.

scoliosis   A sideways curve of the spine that results in an S shape of the back, a common defect in childhood.

sebopsoriasis   Severe form of dandruff (not called psoriasis), usually in the scalp.

seborrheic dermatitis   A common, long-term inflammatory skin disease marked by dry or moist, greasy scales and yellowish crusts.

seroma   A collection of serum (thin watery fluid), usually following a surgical incision.

sodium   Salt.

sohygm(o)   A word part denoting the pulse of blood pressure, as in *sphygomomometer*, an instrument for measuring blood pressure.

sphincter   A muscle that encircles a duct, a tube, or an orifice.

spondylosis   A condition of the spine marked by stiffness of a vertebral joint.

subarachnoid   Underneath the arachnoid membrane—the delicate fibrous middle of three coverings of the central nervous system.

subdigastric   A prominent lymph node lying below the muscle of the posterior belly.

supine   Lying face upward.

supraclavicular   Pertaining to the area of the body above the clavicle, or collarbone.

supraglottis   Anatomic portion above the vocal cords including the epiglottis.

surgery   A branch of medicine concerned with diseases and conditions requiring or amenable to operative or manual procedures; the work performed by a surgeon.

surrogate   One that serves as a substitute.

symptomatology   All of the symptoms which are present in a particular illness.

synovia   A clear, sticky fluid which acts as a lubricant for many joints, bursae, and tendons.

systolic (blood pressure)   The force with which the blood is pumped when the heart muscle is contracting.

telangiectatic   Having a vascular lesion formed by location of a group of small blood vessels.

thallium   A soft, bluish-white metal element with some nonmetallic chemical properties.

thorac(o)   A word element denoting the chest or thorax, as in thoracotomy, a surgical incision of the chest wall.

thromboid   Like or resembling a clot.

trabeculated   Bladder characterized by thick walls and hypertrophied muscle bundles.

transluminal   Across or through the space in the interior of a blood vessel or other tubular structure.

trocars   Instruments for withdrawing fluid from a cavity.

trophic   Resulting from the interruption of nerve supply.

turbinates   The bony edges within the nose.

tympanomeatal   Pertaining to a flap created in the ear canal to the eardrum for ear surgery.

tympanoplasty   Plastic surgery to repair a damaged eardrum.

ulcerate   To form an ulcer.

urinalysis   Analysis of the urine.

urology   Field of medicine specializing in the diagnosis and treatment of disorders and diseases of the male genital system and of the urinary system in both sexes.

varicella   Chickenpox.

vasomotor   Of or relating to the nerves and muscles that control the width of blood vessels.

vasospasm   Contraction of a vessel.

ventricular   Of or relating to a small cavity, as of the brain or heart.

Staff Directory

ALBERT, Louise A., Mrs.
Admin. Assist., Plastic Surgery
Room 241
X-7871

ALBERTSON, Lou
Admin. Assist., Urology
Room 424
X-7904

ALEXANDER, Lawrence, M.D.
Director of Oncology
Room 400
X-7880

AMOS, Mary Louise, M.D.
Oncology
Room 402
X-7882

ANDERSON, Keith, M.D.
Radiology
Room 110
X-7811

AVANI, Nathan, MBA
Associate Director for Business
Room 112
X-7814

AVERY, Sebastian, M.D.
Head & Neck
Room 304
X-7852

BAKER, James, M.D.
Emergency Room
Room 111
X-7888

BARNETT, Daniel, M.D.
Internal Medicine
Room 222
X-7832

BAYNES, Larry
Administrative Office Manager
Room 102
X-7803

BEACH, Mildred
Accountant
Room 107
X-7809

BEDNAR, Andrew, M.D.
Director of Allergy/Immunology
Room 330
X-7845

BODNER, Lester, M.D.
Oncology
Room 401
X-7881

BOLAND, John P., M.D.
Director of Radiology
Room 120
X-7890

CHUNG, Shan, M.D.
Allergy/Immunology
Room 332
X-7847

EADIE, Thomas, M.D.
Cardiovascular Medicine
Room 231
X-7827

EMERSON, James, M.D.
Internal Medicine
Room 225
X-7835

GILL, John
Assist., Administration
Room 101
X-7802

GLAZER, Jean
Admin. Assist., Surgery
Room 414
X-7894

HARRIS, Justine, Ms.
Admin. Assist., Dermatology
Room 350
X-7876

HART, Georgia
Laboratory Director
Room 108
X-7810

KARNS, Janice S., M.D.
Plastic Surgery
Room 242
X-7872

KARNS, Jason K., M.D.
Cardiovascular Medicine
Room 223
X-7828

KOPACKA, Timothy, CPA
Head of Accounting
Room 106
X-7807

LAKOTA, Susan, M.D.
Urology
Room 422
X-7902

LARSON, Alvin K., M.D.
Director of Plastic Surgery
Room 240
X-7870

LAWLER, Connie
Director of Admissions
Room 115
X-7821

LAY, Christine, R.N.
Surgery
Room 412
X-7892

LINCOLN, Daniel, M.D.
Radiology
Room 121
X-7891

LONGTREE, Clayton Lee, M.D.
Director of Dermatology
Room 351
X-7875

McGINTY, Michael, M.D.
Internal Medicine
Room 226
X-7836

MEISKE-ROSE, Sharon, M.D.
Dermatology
Room 352
X-7877

MILLER, Jane, M.D.
Urology
Room 322
X-7842

MOFFETT, Lucille
Admin. Assist., Admissions
Room 116
X-7822

NEHLSON, Patrick, M.D.
Director of Urology
Room 420
X-7875

NEWTON, Edwin, M.D.
Urology
Room 423
X-7875

NOVAK, Steven, M.D.
Chief Administrator
Room 100
X-7801

OASTER, Diane
Admin. Assist., Head & Neck
Room 301
X-7851

O'DELL, Chris, M.D.
Head & Neck
Room 302
X-7852

PATTERSON, Milton, M.D.
Director of Surgery
Room 410
X-7890

PHELPS, Mildred, M.D.
Surgery
Room 411
X-7891

ROBERTS, Neil
Assoc. Admin. for Medicine
Room 200
X-7860

ROE, Louise
Admin. Assist., Oncology
Room 405
X-7884

ROSE, Sharon
Admin. Assist., Accounting
Room 320
X-7840

RYAN, Marge
Pharmacy
Room 109
X-7816

SCOTT, Leslie, Audiologist
Head & Neck
Room 303
X-7853

SHETZER, Carolyn, R.N.
Oncology
Room 404
X-7883

STEVENS, Nancy Ann, R.N.
Internal Medicine
Room 230
X-7825

SZABO, Jeffrey, M.D.
Director of Cardiovascular Med.
Room 231
X-7825

THOMAS, Curt
Admin. Assist., Cardiovascular
Med.
Room 232
X-7826

TYSON, Mildred, Office Assist.
Allergy/Immunology
Room 331
X-7846

VEENSTRA, Nancy, M.D.
Director of Internal Medicine
Room 220
X-7830

WADE, John, M.D.
Urology
Room 320
X-7840

WALLACE, Jackie
Office Assist., Internal Medicine
Room 221
X-7891

WHEELER, Mildred, R.N.
Surgery
Room 415
X-7895

ZHU, Xiao-Lan
Laboratory
Room 110
X-7812

ZISS, Thomas, M.D.
Director of Head & Neck
Room 300
X-7850

Patient Directory

ABRAMS, Leonard
345 Summit Street
Bowling Green, OH 43402-1206
419-555-0177

ANTHONY, Tony K.
346 Third Street
Perrysburg, OH 43451-1543
419-555-8921

BOOK, Cassandra
867 North Front Street
Findlay, OH 45840-1389
419-555-8900

BOULDEN, Henry F.
125 Siesta Avenue
Paulding, OH 45817-2588
419-555-1264

BUCK, Elsie May
2341 Prospect Street
Stony Ridge, OH 43463-5423
419-555-1220

CARNUTTE, Edgar
Rural Route 2
Mount Vernon, OH 43050-2544
419-555-1220

CHURCH, James J.
425 Jefferson Avenue
Toledo, OH 43604-1389
419-555-7865

CICHY, Ronald F.
456 Main Street
Grand Rapids, OH 43522-1008
419-555-0667

COX, Louise A.
1345 Telegraph Road
Monroe, MI 48161-3412
313-555-4477

CROSS, Albert
56 Sixth Street
Maumee, OH 45357-2341
419-555-9167

DAMER, Jane May
300 Avondale Avenue
Toledo, OH 43502-4412
419-555-9912

DAMON, Ashleigh
Damon, Mrs. Louise, Guardian
166 Second Street
Bryan, OH 43506-2234
419-555-9901

DAVIS, Cindy Louise
Route 2
Custar, OH 43511-1002
419-555-9044

DAVIS, Lisa Q.
8934 Mustard Road
Haskins, OH 43524-4501
419-555-8787

DAVIS, Sherry C.
345 Main Street
Cygnet, OH 43513-2100
419-555-1122

DEMOULIN, Evan
2100 Consaul Lane
Toledo, OH 43506-1304
419-555-8342

EHRET, Gail M.
382 Nebraska Avenue
Toledo, OH 43502-1345
419-555-1789

ERICKSON, Bruce
456 East Maumee
Monroe, MI 48161-3413
313-555-4389

FALK, Julia Mae
231 16th Street
Toledo, OH 43524-1567
419-555-8901

FEATHERSTONE, Oscar
5762 Central Avenue
Sylvania, OH 43561-1378
419-555-2278

GATES, Cynthia B.
Route 45
Waterville, OH 43566-1001
419-555-6458

GOAD, Doris S.
675 Sixth Street
Perrysburg, OH 43451-1933
419-555-7329

GOSSMAN, Arthur A.
523 Weston Road
Custar, OH 43511-1009
419-555-3467

HAGGERTY, Pamela C.
111 South Summit
Toledo, OH 43502-1890
419-555-1723

HARRIS, Jason K.
457 South Luke Avenue
Wallbridge, OH 43465-1437
419-555-7873

HATFIELD, Robert D.
67 Main Street
Luckey, OH 43443-2896
419-555-2771

HUGHES, Marcey
451 First Street
Maumee, OH 43537-2341
419-555-0078

IVEY, Leonard J.
311 Summit Street
Toledo, OH 43502-1981
419-555-2244

JONES, Clinton
405 Madison Avenue
Toledo, OH 43504-1300
419-555-5621

KAUFMAN, Otto
1345 Telegraph Road
Monroe, MI 48161-3289
313-555-4366

LAMBERT, Glenna
Route 45
Findley, OH 45840-1287
419-555-7751

LEE, Hyung Il
420 Madison Avenue
Toledo, OH 43404-1309
419-555-2233

LONGWORTH, Kyle
3350 Anthony Wayne Trail
Maumee, OH 43537-4308
419-555-8811

LOPEZ, Angela
Box 56
Custar, OH 43524-3617
419-555-9067

LOPEZ, Marilyn D.
Route 6
Grand Rapids, OH 43522-2244
419-555-0909

MCFADDEN, Jean D.
222 Lake Road
Jackson, MI 49204-2211
517-555-0177

NEUMAN, Phil
23 Maumee Street
Defiance, OH 43512-1409
517-555-2244

OTTO, William Q.
87 Lotus Avenue
Bryan, OH 43506-1509
419-555-6530

POWELL, Deborah S.
1200 South Street
Maumee, OH 43537-2216
419-555-0089

RAE, Diane S.
940 South Detroit Road
Toledo, OH 43403-3456
419-555-9713

ST. JOHN, April
100 Lincoln Avenue
Fostoria, OH 44830-1508
419-555-9922

SAWAIA, Lucas K.
4925 Jackson Road
Toledo, OH 43513-3564
419-555-5175

SHOEMAKER, Frances L., Mrs.
678 Secor Road
Toledo, OH 43402-2276
419-555-1776

STARK, Stanley
101 Carmel Circle
Montpelier, OH 43543-2008
419-555-9045

TRUMBLE, Nancy K.
4567 Shafer Street
Delta, OH 43515-1689
419-555-5643

VARGAS, Joseph L.
Route 23
West Unity, OH 43570-3106
419-555-7723

WADE, Paul S.
567 Bay Boulevard
Port Clinton, OH 43452-1137
419-555-2317

WALEN, Peter H.
778 Oak Street
Swanton, OH 43558-1326
419-555-5840

ZOLLMAN, Doris A.
1289 Pine Drive
Rossford, OH 43460-4591
419-555-4423

Medicines and Medical Terminology Chart

This form will serve as a practical reference as you work through the text. Remove the page from your text and use it to record definitions of medicines and medical terms that are not found in the Glossary.

Job Number / Medicine/Term	Definition
Job Number Medicine/Term	Definition
Job Number Medicine/Term	Definition
Job Number Medicine/Term	Definition
Job Number Medicine/Term	Definition
Job Number Medicine/Term	Definition
Job Number Medicine/Term	Definition
Job Number Medicine/Term	Definition
Job Number Medicine/Term	Definition
Job Number Medicine/Term	Definition
Job Number Medicine/Term	Definition
Job Number Medicine/Term	Definition
Job Number Medicine/Term	Definition
Job Number Medicine/Term	Definition

Technical Data Chart

Technical data, especially numbers, symbols, and abbreviations, are common in medical documents and must be precise. Remove this chart and record on it the phrases, abbreviations, and special formats that you frequently type, as shown in the example.

Be sure to indicate spacing accurately. Refer to the chart whenever necessary to verify capitalization, punctuation, and so on.

Job	Technical Data
20	graft x 3 in 1992 STAT PTCA 20 mg 1 tablet P.O. t. i. d.
21	11 MET. and > 85%

Job	Technical Data

Job Profile Chart

UNIT 1: ADMISSIONS OFFICE

Use this Job Profile Chart to help track your production work. Remove the form and record the submission or instructor approval date for each job in the appropriate column. Your instructor may indicate which jobs, if any, are to be omitted.

Save this chart for future reference. As jobs are later retrieved and revised, you may refer to this list for job numbers and other information.

Job Number	Omit	Job Description	Submission/ Instructor Approval Date
01		Incoming-Patient Registration Form	
02		Composed Report	
03		Merged Letter	
04		Memo	
05		Appointment Schedule	
06		Policy for Recording & Honoring Living Wills	
07		Dictated Memo	
08		Letter	
09		Patient Information Form	
10		Dictated Memo	

Job Profile Chart

UNIT 2: HEAD AND NECK UNIT

Use this Job Profile Chart to help track your production work. Remove the form and record the submission or instructor approval date for each job in the appropriate column. Your instructor may indicate which jobs, if any, are to be omitted.

Save this chart for future reference. As jobs are later retrieved and revised, you may refer to this list for job numbers and other information.

Job Number	Omit	Job Description	Submission/ Instructor Approval Date
11		Head and Neck Unit Letterhead	
12		Summary of ENG Findings	
13		Head and Neck Unit Memo Heading	
14		Memo	
15		Operative Report	
16a–f		Merged Letters	
17		Authorization for Release of Medical Information	
18a–c		Authorization for Release of Medical Information	
19		Dictated Consultation Letter	
20		Pathology Report	
21		Memorial Hospital Radiology Report	
22		Patient Data File	

Job Profile Chart

Use this Job Profile Chart to help track your production work. Remove the form and record the submission or instructor approval date for each job in the appropriate column. Your instructor may indicate which jobs, if any, are to be omitted.

Save this chart for future reference. As jobs are later retrieved and revised, you may refer to this list for job numbers and other information.

Job Number	Omit	Job Description	Submission/ Instructor Approval Date
23		Cardiovascular Medicine Unit Letterhead	
24		Exercise Test Consent Form	
25		Discharge Summary	
26		Exercise Treadmill with Echo Report	
27		Stress Echo Report	
28		Dobutamine Thallium Test Information Form	
29		Dictated Consultation Letter	
30		Return Office Visit Form	
31		Return Visit Report	
32		Dictated Consultation Letter	
33		History and Physical Report	
34		Operative Report	

Job Profile Chart

Use this Job Profile Chart to help track your production work. Remove the form and record the submission or instructor approval date for each job in the appropriate column. Your instructor may indicate which jobs, if any, are to be omitted.

Save this chart for future reference. As jobs are later retrieved and revised, you may refer to this list for job numbers and other information.

Job Number	Omit	Job Description	Submission/ Instructor Approval Date
35		Plastic Surgery Letterhead	
36a–b		Dictated Patient Data File	
37		Operative Consent	
38		Plastic Surgery Unit Memo Heading	
39		Memo	
40a–f		Merge Letter	
41a–b		Authorization for Release of Medical Information	
42a–c		Operative Consent	
43a–b		Dictated Patient Data File	
44a–b		Dictated Patient Data File	
45		Letter	

Job Profile Chart

UNIT 5: ALLERGY/IMMUNOLOGY UNIT

Use this Job Profile Chart to help track your production work. Remove the form and record the submission or instructor approval date for each job in the appropriate column. Your instructor may indicate which jobs, if any, are to be omitted.

Save this chart for future reference. As jobs are later retrieved and revised, you may refer to this list for job numbers and other information.

Job Number	Omit	Job Description	Submission/ Instructor Approval Date
46		Allergy/Immunology Unit Letterhead	
47		Allergy/Immunology Unit Memo Heading	
48		Release from Waiting Time	
49		Dictated Consultation Letter	
50		Dictated Memo	
51		Influenza (Flu) Vaccine Consent	
52		Dictated Consultation Letter	
53		Allergy Skin Test Form	
54		Revised Consultation Letter	
55		Dictated Consultation Letter	
56		Radiology Report	
57		Dictated Memo	

Job Profile Chart

Use this Job Profile Chart to help track your production work. Remove the form and record the submission or instructor approval date for each job in the appropriate column. Your instructor may indicate which jobs, if any, are to be omitted.

Save this chart for future reference. As jobs are later retrieved and revised, you may refer to this list for job numbers and other information.

Job Number	Omit	Job Description	Submission/ Instructor Approval Date
58		Urology Unit Letterhead	
59		Dictated Consultation Letter	
60		Operative Report	
61		Form	
62		Handwritten Operative Report	
63		Prostate Biopsy Form	
64		Dictated Consultation Letter	
65		Patient Data File	

Job Profile Chart

Use this Job Profile Chart to help track your production work. Remove the form and record the submission or instructor approval date for each job in the appropriate column. Your instructor may indicate which jobs, if any, are to be omitted.

Save this chart for future reference. As jobs are later retrieved and revised, you may refer to this list for job numbers and other information.

Job Number	Omit	Job Description	Submission/ Instructor Approval Date
66		Surgery Unit Letterhead	
67		Dictated Consultation Letter	
68		Operative Report	
69		Medical Information Form	
70		Dictated Letter	
71		Operative Report	
72		Information Form Letter	
73		Unit Memo Heading	
74		Dictated Memo	
75		Patient Data File	
76		Pathology Report	
77		Patient Data File	

Job Profile Chart

UNIT 8: ONCOLOGY UNIT

Use this Job Profile Chart to help track your production work. Remove the form and record the submission or instructor approval date for each job in the appropriate column. Your instructor may indicate which jobs, if any, are to be omitted.

Save this chart for future reference. As jobs are later retrieved and revised, you may refer to this list for job numbers and other information.

Job Number	Omit	Job Description	Submission/ Instructor Approval Date
78		Oncology Unit Letterhead	
79		Form Letter	
80		Operative Report	
81		Announcement	
82		Unit Memo Heading	
83		Handwritten Memo	
84		Dictated Consultation Letter	
85		Labels	
86		Dictated Consultation Letter	
87		Table	
88		Dictated Consultation Letter	
89		Pathology Report	
90		Dictated Consultation Letter	
91		Composed Report	
92		Dictated Consultation Letter	

Job Profile Chart

UNIT 9: DERMATOLOGY UNIT

Use this Job Profile Chart to help track your production work. Remove the form and record the submission or instructor approval date for each job in the appropriate column. Your instructor may indicate which jobs, if any, are to be omitted.

Save this chart for future reference. As jobs are later retrieved and revised, you may refer to this list for job numbers and other information.

Job Number	Omit	Job Description	Submission/ Instructor Approval Date
93		Dermatology Unit Letterhead	
94		Consultation Letter	
95		Patient Data File	
96		Consultation Letter	
97		Patient Data File	
98		Dermatology Unit Memo Heading	
99		Memo	
100		Patient's Rights and Responsibilities	
101		Composed Memo	
102		Dictated Consultation Letter	
103		Patient Data File	
104		Memo	
105		Table	
106		Consultation Letter	
107		Patient Data File	

Job Profile Chart

Use this Job Profile Chart to help track your production work. Remove the form and record the submission or instructor approval date for each job in the appropriate column. Your instructor may indicate which jobs, if any, are to be omitted.

Save this chart for future reference. As jobs are later retrieved and revised, you may refer to this list for job numbers and other information.

Job Number	Omit	Job Description	Submission/ Instructor Approval Date
108		Internal Medicine Unit Letterhead	
109		Dictated Letter	
110		Physical Examination Report	
111		Rough-Draft Consultation Report	
112		Composed Report	
113a–c		Patient Data File	
114		Announcement Letter	
115		Form	
116		Radiology Report	

INDEX

Admissions unit, 16–27
Addresses
  names, 18, 33
AIDS awareness, 131–132
Allergy/immunology unit, 66–77
Allergy skin test form, 73–74
Announcement, 102
  letter, 131
Apostrophe, for possession, 26
Appointment schedule, 20
Attachments, 26
Audiologist, 28
Authorization for release of
    medical information, 34, 35,
    63

Capitalization,
  first letter in medications, 87
  with geographic name, 119
Cardiac catheterization, 51
Cardiovascular medicine unit,
    40–55
Commas,
  after introductory phrases, 48
  use of, in expressions, 48
  with name used in direct
    address, 115
Composed memo, 117
Composed reports, 17, 110, 130
Consultant pharmacist, 78
Consultation letter, 84–85
Consultation reports, 35, 69,
    72–73, 75–76, 79, 87–89,
    104, 105, 107, 108–110, 113,
    114, 118, 121, 127, 129
Coronary angioplasty, 48
Cystoscopy, 80
Cytotechnologist, 86

Dates,
  in headings, 43
  preceding month, 69, 75
Dermatology unit, 112–121
Discharge summary reports, 43–44
Distribution list, 22, 27
Document codes, 17, 30
Dobutamine thallium test
    information, 47

EKG technician, 40
ENG test, 30
Esq (Esquire), 123
Exercise test consent form, 42
Exercise treadmill with echo
    report, 45
Extracorporeal shockwave
    lithotripsy, 81

Focus on Medical Careers
  audiologist, 28
  consultant pharmacist, 78
  cytotechnologist, 86
  EKG technician, 40
  medical assistant, 16
  medical transcriptionist, 112
  pathologist assistant, 56
  physician's assistant, 122
  radiographer/sonographer, 98
  respiratory therapist, 66
Formatting (See Procedures
    Manual for formatting
    letters, memos, forms, and
    reports.)
  dates in headings, 43
  letterhead, 18, 29
  medications, 43, 49, 90, 114
  memo heading, 19, 30
  paragraphs, 32
  physician's names, degrees, 22,
    43, 48, 51
Form letters, 18, 95, 99–102
Forms
  AIDS awareness, 131–132
  allergy skin test, 73–74
  appointment schedule, 20
  authorization for release of
    medical information, 34,
    35, 63
  Dobutamine thallium test
    information, 47
  exercise test consent, 42
  incoming patient information, 24
  incoming patient registration, 17
  influenza (FLU) vaccine
    consent, 70–71
  medical information, 92
  operative consent, 59–60, 63
  patient information, 24–26
  patient rights and
    responsibilities, 116–117
  policy for recording and
    handling living wills, 21–22
  postoperative information for
    the extracorporeal
    shockwave lithotripsy
    patient, 81
  prostate biopsy, 83
  release from waiting time, 68
  return visit, 49–50

Head and neck unit, 28–39
History and physical report,
    52–53
Hyphen,
  after a prefix ending in *i*, 57

with adjective before noun, 87
with compound adverbs, 124

Incoming patient information
  form, 24–26
Incoming patient registration
  form, 17
Influenza (FLU) vaccine consent
  form, 70–71
Inside address, 18
Internal medicine unit, 122–133
Is That a Fact, 17, 20, 26, 30, 31,
    35, 38, 41, 46, 51, 58, 62, 64,
    67, 69, 73, 77, 79, 83, 85, 89,
    91, 95, 96, 102, 104, 106,
    110, 115, 118, 119, 121, 126,
    129, 132

Labels, 104
Language arts
  addresses, names in, 18
  apostrophe, for possession, 27
  capitalization,
    first letter of medications,
    87
  with geographic name, 119
  commas,
    after introductory phrases, 48
    use of, in expressions, 48
    with a name used in direct
      address, 115
  dates,
    in headings, 43
    preceding month, 69, 75
  figures and symbols, rather than
    words, 36
  hyphen,
    after a prefix ending in *i*, 57
    with adjective before noun, 87
    with compound adverbs, 124
  medical terms and phrases, 36,
    49, 72, 90, 114
  ordinal numbers, 23
  paragraphs,
    continuing to next page, 32
    headings, 52
  parentheses to enclose numbers,
    87
Laparoscropic cholecystectomy
    surgery, 90
Letterhead, 18, 29
Letters
  announcement, 131
  block 18, 64
  dictated, 48, 51, 84, 93, 123–124
  form, 18, 95, 99
  letterhead, 18, 29

merge, 18, 33, 62
RE: (Subject), 48
salutation, 33
rough draft, 23–24

Medical assistant, 16
Medical information form, 92
Medical terms and phrases, 36, 49, 72, 90, 114
Medical transcriptionist, 112
Merge letters, 18, 33, 62
Memos,
   composed, 117
   dictated, 22, 27, 69, 77, 96
   formatting heading, 19, 30
   handwritten, 31, 103, 115, 119
   rough draft, 61
Miz, 35
Ms, 33
MUGA test, 49

Oncology unit, 98–111
Operative consent form, 59–60, 63
Operative report, 32, 80, 90–91, 93–94, 100–102
   handwritten, 82
Ordinal numbers, 23

Parentheses to enclose numbers, 87
Paragraphs,
   continuing to next page, 32
   headings, 52
Pathologist assistant, 56
Pathology report, 36, 97, 107–108
Patient data files, 38, 85, 97, 114, 115, 119, 121
   dictated, 57–58, 63
   handwritten, 97, 130
Patient information form, 24–26

Patient rights and responsibilities, 116–117
Perennial allergic rhinitis, 75
Periurethral collagen injection, 80
Physical examination report, 124–126
Physician's assistant, 122
Physician's names and degrees, 43, 48, 51
Plastic surgery unit, 56–65
Policy for recording and handling living wills form, 21
Portfolio, 27, 39, 55, 65, 77, 85, 97, 111, 121, 133
Postoperative report for extra corporeal shockwave lithotripsy, 81–82
Procedures Manual, 1–15
Prostate biopsy form, 83

Radiographer/sonographer, 98
Radiology report, 37, 76–77, 133
RE: (Subject), 48
Reference initials, 58
Release for medical information, 63
Release from waiting times form, 68
Reports,
   composed, 17, 100, 130
   consultation, 35, 69, 72–73, 75–76, 79, 87–89, 104, 105 107, 108–110, 111, 113, 114, 118, 121, 127–129
   discharge summary, 43–44
   exercise treadmill with echo, 45
   history and physical, 52
   operative, 32, 80, 90–91, 93–94, 100–102
     handwritten, 82

pathology, 36, 97, 107–108
patient data files, 38, 85, 97, 114, 115, 119, 121
   dictated, 57–58, 63
   handwritten, 97, 130
physical examination, 124–126
postoperative, 81, 82
radiology, 37, 76–77, 133
return visit, 49–50
stress text echo, 46
summary of ENG findings, 30
Respiratory therapist, 66
Return visit form, 49
Rough draft letters, 18, 30, 62

Salutations,
   miz (Ms), 35
   young girl, 33
Sonographer, 98
Stress echo report, 46
Summary of ENG findings, 30
Surgery unit, 86–97

Tables, 20, 106, 120
Terms to Know, 16, 28, 40, 56, 66, 78, 86, 98, 112, 122

Units
   admissions, 16–27
   allergy/immunology, 66–77
   cardiovascular medicine, 40–55
   dermatology, 112–121
   head and neck, 28–39
   internal medicine, 122–133
   oncology, 98–111
   plastic surgery, 56–65
   surgery, 86–97
   urology, 78–85
Urology unit, 78–85